The Thinking Habit

Why the Mind Repeats What It Learns

Table of Contents

Introduction

The Habitual Mind

Human beings like to believe that they think freely, consciously, and independently. We often imagine the mind as a rational engine—evaluating information, weighing evidence, and arriving at conclusions through deliberate effort. Yet most thinking does not occur this way. In reality, the majority of our thoughts are automatic, repetitive, and deeply shaped by what we have already learned. The mind, more than a neutral processor, is a habit-forming system.

The habitual nature of thinking explains why people return to the same ideas, interpretations, and conclusions again and again—even when circumstances change or evidence challenges them. Thoughts repeat not because they are always correct, but because they are familiar. The brain prioritizes efficiency over accuracy, conserving energy by reusing established mental pathways rather than creating new ones. Over time, these repeated pathways become the default way we perceive the world.

Thinking, therefore, is not merely an act—it is a pattern. From early childhood onward, the mind absorbs information through repetition: words spoken by caregivers, emotional reactions to experiences, cultural norms, rewards, punishments, and social approval. Each repetition strengthens a particular way of interpreting reality. Eventually, these interpretations no longer feel learned; they feel natural, obvious, and unquestionable. What we call "common sense" is often nothing more than deeply reinforced habit.

This is why two people can observe the same event and arrive at entirely different conclusions. Their minds are not reacting to the event itself, but to the patterns they have learned to associate with similar situations in the past. Memory, emotion, and expectation work together to guide perception long before conscious reasoning begins. By the time we believe we are "thinking," much of the work has already been done automatically.

The habitual mind is not a flaw; it is a survival mechanism. In an unpredictable world, repetition creates stability. Familiar thoughts provide comfort, coherence, and a sense of identity. They reduce uncertainty and protect us from the mental strain of constant analysis. However, the same mechanism that allows us to function efficiently can also trap us in rigid thinking, distorted beliefs, and repeated errors.

Modern life intensifies this effect. Repeated exposure to the same messages—through education systems, media cycles, social environments, and digital platforms—reinforces certain ideas while marginalizing others. Over time, repetition alone can create belief. The mind begins to confuse familiarity with truth, confidence with accuracy, and repetition with evidence. Once a thought becomes habitual, it resists change not because it is strong, but because it is comfortable.

Understanding the habitual nature of thinking is essential for intellectual growth. Without awareness, we mistake conditioned responses for independent judgment. We defend ideas as if they were self-chosen, even when they were inherited, absorbed, or reinforced without conscious consent. This illusion of autonomy makes critical thinking difficult, as questioning a habitual thought often feels like questioning one's identity.

This book begins with a simple but powerful premise: the mind repeats what it learns. Thoughts follow grooves carved by experience, emotion, language, and reinforcement. If those grooves remain unexamined, thinking becomes predictable. If they are understood, they can be reshaped.

The goal of this book is not to eliminate habits of thought—such a task would be neither possible nor desirable. Instead, it aims to make them visible. Awareness transforms unconscious repetition into conscious choice. When we recognize how thoughts are formed, stored, and reinforced, we gain the ability to intervene. We can slow down reflexive thinking, introduce reflection, and replace automatic responses with deliberate reasoning.

Throughout the chapters that follow, we will explore how thinking habits are created, why they persist, and how they influence perception, emotion, and behavior. We will examine the role of memory, language, social influence, emotion, and attention in shaping the mental patterns that govern daily life. Most importantly, we will address how these patterns can be adjusted—not through force, but through understanding.

The habitual mind is not fixed. It is adaptive, plastic, and responsive to training. Just as repeated exposure once shaped our thinking without permission, intentional practice can reshape it with purpose. By learning how the mind repeats what it learns, we begin the process of learning how to think differently—not occasionally, but habitually.

This book is an invitation to observe your own thinking patterns with honesty and precision. In doing so, you move from being governed by mental habits to becoming their architect.

Chapter 1

Thinking as a Habit, Not a Talent

From early education to everyday conversation, thinking is often treated as a natural talent—something some people simply possess more than others. We speak of individuals as "smart," "sharp," or "quick thinkers," while others are labeled as slow, unfocused, or incapable of deep reasoning. This framing suggests that thinking ability is largely fixed, inherited, and unevenly distributed. Yet this belief overlooks a more fundamental truth: thinking is not primarily a talent. It is a habit.

A habit is a behavior strengthened through repetition. The more it is practiced, the more automatic it becomes. Thinking follows the same principle. People do not think well because they were born with superior minds; they think well because they have repeatedly engaged in certain mental behaviors—questioning assumptions, examining alternatives, reflecting before reacting, and tolerating uncertainty. Over time, these behaviors solidify into patterns that appear effortless and innate.

When thinking is mistaken for talent, it becomes mystified. Those who struggle with reasoning often assume the limitation lies within them rather than in their training or environment. This belief discourages growth. If thinking is a gift, then effort seems pointless. If thinking is a habit, effort becomes the pathway to improvement. This shift in perspective is not merely motivational; it is structural. It changes how we understand learning, intelligence, and personal development.

The mind does not default to careful reasoning. It defaults to efficiency. The brain's primary goal is to conserve energy while maintaining functionality. Analytical thinking is slow, effortful, and metabolically expensive. Habitual thinking, by contrast, is fast and economical. It relies on familiar mental shortcuts developed through repetition. These shortcuts are not inherently flawed—they allow us to navigate daily life without paralysis—but they are often mistaken for intelligence itself.

What appears as intellectual sharpness is frequently the result of practiced mental routines. A person who quickly identifies patterns, draws conclusions, or articulates ideas fluently is often someone who has rehearsed those processes repeatedly. Exposure, feedback, and correction gradually refine their thinking until it becomes automatic. To an observer, this looks like natural ability. In reality, it is conditioned competence.

This understanding also explains why intelligence can vary dramatically across contexts. A person may demonstrate remarkable clarity in one domain and confusion in another. Talent cannot explain this inconsistency; habit can. Where thinking has been practiced, it flows. Where it has not, it falters. The mind performs best in areas where it has learned what to notice, how to interpret information, and which questions to ask.

Educational systems often reinforce the talent myth by rewarding correct answers rather than thoughtful processes. Students learn to repeat information rather than examine it. Those who adapt quickly are praised as intelligent, while others internalize the belief that they are incapable thinkers. In reality, many students simply have not been taught how to think; they have been taught what to recall. Repetition still occurs—but it reinforces memorization instead of reasoning.

Social environments further entrench this pattern. Families, cultures, and communities model specific ways of interpreting events, assigning meaning, and responding emotionally. These interpretations are absorbed long before critical thinking skills develop. By adulthood, many beliefs feel self-evident not because they have been examined, but because they have been repeated. The habit has replaced inquiry.

Viewing thinking as a habit also reveals why change is difficult. Habits resist disruption. They provide predictability and psychological comfort. Challenging a familiar thought pattern creates cognitive discomfort, often experienced as confusion, irritation, or defensiveness. This discomfort is frequently misinterpreted as evidence that the new idea is wrong, rather than unfamiliar. As a result, the mind retreats to what it knows.

Recognizing thinking as a habit reframes intellectual growth as a process of training rather than transformation. One does not "become smarter" overnight; one gradually develops better thinking routines. These routines include slowing down automatic judgments, separating emotion from evaluation, seeking evidence rather than affirmation, and remaining open to revision. Each repetition strengthens the habit.

This chapter establishes a foundation for the rest of the book. By rejecting the myth of thinking as talent, we open the door to responsibility and possibility. If thinking is habitual, it can be reshaped. If it can be reshaped, it can be improved. The question is no longer who is capable of good thinking, but what kind of thinking is being practiced—consciously or unconsciously—every day.

Understanding this distinction is the first step toward mastering the thinking habit.

The Difference Between Thinking and Intelligence

Thinking and intelligence are often used interchangeably, yet they describe fundamentally different aspects of the human mind. Intelligence is commonly understood as capacity: the raw potential of the brain to process information, recognize patterns, store memory, and solve problems. Thinking, by contrast, is a process: the active use of that capacity through habits, strategies, and deliberate mental behavior. Confusing the two leads to widespread misunderstanding about learning, ability, and personal growth.

Intelligence refers to what the mind can do under optimal conditions. It includes cognitive resources such as memory range, processing speed, abstract reasoning potential, and neural efficiency. These capacities vary among individuals due to genetics, early development, health, and neurological factors. Intelligence sets the upper boundaries of what is possible, but it does not determine how frequently or effectively those possibilities are used. A powerful engine does not guarantee skilled driving.

Thinking describes how the mind is actually used in daily life. It involves attention, interpretation, judgment, reflection, and decision-making. Thinking is shaped by repetition, environment, training, and reinforcement. Two individuals with similar intelligence levels can demonstrate radically different thinking quality depending on how they habitually engage their minds. One may question assumptions and examine evidence, while the other reacts automatically and relies on unexamined beliefs.

This distinction explains a common observation: highly intelligent individuals often make poor decisions, while others of average intelligence display remarkable clarity and wisdom. Intelligence alone does not protect against bias, emotional reasoning, or faulty assumptions. Without disciplined thinking habits, intelligence can amplify error rather than prevent it. The mind simply becomes more efficient at defending mistaken conclusions.

Thinking requires effort, while intelligence exists passively. Intelligence does not demand engagement; thinking does. The brain naturally seeks efficiency and comfort, defaulting to familiar patterns rather than analytical rigor. As a result, even individuals with high intellectual capacity frequently rely on shortcuts, stereotypes, and reflexive judgments unless they have trained themselves to think otherwise. Thinking well is not automatic; it is practiced.

Another critical difference lies in flexibility. Intelligence is relatively stable across adulthood, while thinking is adaptable throughout life. People rarely experience dramatic increases in raw intelligence, but they can significantly improve how they think. Learning to slow down, to question first impressions, to tolerate ambiguity, and to revise beliefs can transform mental performance without changing cognitive capacity. This plasticity makes thinking a skill rather than a trait.

Educational systems often obscure this difference by equating intelligence with performance. Test scores, grades, and rankings reward recall and speed more than reflection and reasoning. Students learn to associate intelligence with correct answers instead of sound thinking processes. Those who perform poorly may conclude they lack intelligence, when in reality they have not developed effective thinking habits. The damage is not intellectual but psychological.

Thinking also involves values and discipline, which intelligence does not. A person may be capable of complex reasoning yet choose not to engage in it. Thinking well requires patience, humility, and willingness to confront uncertainty. These qualities are not measures of intelligence; they are habits of character. Without them, intelligence remains underutilized.

Emotions further separate thinking from intelligence. Intelligence does not regulate emotion, but thinking must. Emotional reactions often precede conscious thought, shaping interpretation and judgment. Skilled thinking involves recognizing emotional influence and adjusting reasoning accordingly. Intelligent individuals who lack emotional awareness may rationalize feelings rather than examine facts, mistaking intensity for insight.

Social conditioning also plays a role. Intelligence operates internally, but thinking is socially trained. Cultural narratives, authority figures, and group norms teach people what to think long before they learn how to think. Over time, repeated beliefs feel self-evident. Intelligence may enable complex justification of these beliefs, but only disciplined thinking can question them.

The speed of thinking is another misleading factor. Fast responses are often praised as signs of intelligence, yet speed frequently reflects habit rather than depth. Slow thinking allows for evaluation, comparison, and correction. Intelligence supports both fast and slow thinking, but habit determines which mode dominates. Many errors arise not from lack of intelligence, but from thinking too quickly.

Problem-solving highlights the difference clearly. Intelligence supplies tools; thinking determines how they are used. Faced with a problem, intelligence offers potential strategies, but thinking selects, applies, and evaluates them. Poor thinking misapplies intelligence, repeating ineffective approaches despite evidence. Good thinking adapts.

This distinction has ethical implications. Intelligence can be used to manipulate, deceive, or exploit if thinking lacks moral reflection. Thinking integrates consequences, empathy, and long-term impact. Intelligence alone is neutral; thinking gives it direction. History repeatedly shows that high intelligence without reflective thinking can cause immense harm.

Importantly, thinking improves through feedback, not through praise of intelligence. When individuals are rewarded for effortful reasoning rather than innate ability, they develop resilience and curiosity. Viewing thinking as trainable encourages growth, while viewing intelligence as fixed discourages it. The belief system surrounding intelligence shapes thinking habits themselves.

Ultimately, intelligence is the capacity to think, but thinking is the choice to use that capacity well. One determines potential; the other determines outcome. A mind rich in intelligence but poor in thinking remains reactive, biased, and predictable. A mind trained in thinking, even with modest intelligence, can be insightful, adaptive, and wise.

Recognizing this distinction also reshapes how society defines success and competence. In workplaces, intelligence is often assumed based on credentials, verbal fluency, or technical knowledge, while actual thinking quality remains unexamined. Decisions are then made by those who appear intelligent rather than those who reason carefully. Over time, organizations suffer from repeated strategic errors not because they lack intelligent people, but because habitual thinking goes unchallenged. Groupthink, overconfidence, and unchecked assumptions thrive in environments that confuse intellect with insight.

Thinking manifests most clearly under pressure. When time is limited or stakes are high, habitual thinking dominates. Intelligence does not automatically intervene to correct flawed reactions. Instead, the mind falls back on whatever patterns have been practiced most frequently. This is why training matters more than raw ability. Pilots, surgeons, and emergency responders rely on drilled thinking patterns, not spontaneous intelligence, to function effectively in critical moments. Their competence is habitual, not accidental.

The role of curiosity further highlights the difference. Intelligence does not guarantee curiosity. Some highly intelligent individuals lose interest in questioning once they achieve mastery or recognition. Thinking, however, depends on sustained curiosity: the willingness to explore uncertainty and admit incomplete understanding. Without curiosity, intelligence becomes static, serving existing beliefs rather than expanding them. Habitual thinking either nurtures or suppresses this exploratory impulse.

Mistakes provide another revealing contrast. Intelligence can hide errors by producing convincing explanations, while good thinking exposes them early. Poor thinking resists correction because it is invested in being right. Effective thinking values accuracy over ego. This difference explains why some intelligent individuals repeat the same mistakes for years, while others steadily improve. Learning depends less on intelligence than on how one responds to error.

The modern information environment makes this distinction even more critical. Access to vast knowledge rewards intelligence with speed and breadth, but it also amplifies shallow thinking. Algorithms deliver repeated information that aligns with prior beliefs, reinforcing mental habits without requiring analysis. Intelligence may enable rapid consumption, but only disciplined thinking can evaluate credibility, detect manipulation, and integrate information meaningfully. In an age of abundance, thinking quality matters more than intellectual capacity.

Self-awareness is central to thinking but peripheral to intelligence. Intelligence can operate without awareness of its own limits. Thinking requires meta-cognition: the ability to observe one's own reasoning. This includes recognizing bias, uncertainty, and emotional influence. Without meta-cognition, intelligence functions blindly, confident but unchecked. Thinking turns the mind into both participant and observer.

The development of thinking habits begins early but remains changeable. Children are often praised for being smart instead of for thinking carefully. This praise conditions them to protect an image of intelligence rather than develop thinking skills. Over time, fear of appearing unintelligent discourages questioning and experimentation. Reframing success around thinking effort rather than intellectual identity fosters resilience and growth.

At a societal level, confusing intelligence with thinking contributes to polarization. Intelligent arguments can be constructed for nearly any position. Without shared standards of thinking, debate becomes a contest of rhetorical skill rather than reasoning. Thinking emphasizes evidence, coherence, and openness to revision. Intelligence alone does not. Progress depends on thinking norms, not intellectual hierarchy.

Ultimately, intelligence is a resource, while thinking is a practice. Resources unused produce nothing. Practice shapes outcomes. The most reliable predictor of sound judgment is not intelligence level, but consistency of reflective thinking. This truth empowers individuals. Regardless of starting point, anyone can improve how they think. The mind is not limited by talent as much as it is guided by habit. This distinction defines the difference between potential and intellectual reality.

How Repetition Shapes Mental Processes

Repetition is one of the most powerful forces shaping the human mind. Long before conscious reasoning develops, the brain learns by repeated exposure. Sounds, images, emotional reactions, words, and behaviors are absorbed not because they are analyzed, but because they occur again and again. Over time, repetition transforms experience into expectation and action into instinct. What we think, how we interpret events, and how we respond to the world are largely products of what the mind has encountered most frequently.

At a neurological level, repetition strengthens connections between neurons. When a thought, perception, or behavior is repeated, the neural pathways involved become more efficient. Signals travel faster, require less energy, and activate more automatically. This process allows the brain to function with speed and economy, but it also means that frequently repeated mental processes come to dominate awareness. The brain becomes skilled not at what is true or useful, but at what is familiar.

This mechanism explains why first impressions matter so deeply. Initial experiences lay down early patterns that repetition later reinforces. If an early interpretation of an event is repeated through memory, conversation, or emotional recall, it becomes a stable mental reference point. Even when new information appears, the mind tends to interpret it through existing patterns rather than revise them.

Repetition, not evidence, becomes the organizing principle of thought.

Mental repetition does not require conscious intention. Internal dialogue repeats narratives about identity, ability, and expectation without deliberate choice. Thoughts such as "this always happens," "I am not good at this," or "people cannot be trusted" often originate from repeated experiences rather than reasoned conclusions. Each repetition reinforces the narrative until it feels self-evident. The mind mistakes frequency for validity.

Emotion intensifies the effects of repetition. Experiences charged with fear, pleasure, shame, or reward are more likely to be mentally replayed. Each replay strengthens the emotional and cognitive association, making similar future situations trigger the same response automatically. Over time, emotional repetition trains the mind to anticipate outcomes before they occur, shaping perception itself. The mind does not merely remember; it predicts based on habit.

Language plays a central role in reinforcing mental processes. Words provide structure to experience, and repeated phrases become cognitive shortcuts. Labels simplify complexity, allowing the mind to categorize quickly. However, repeated language also limits perception. Once something is labeled, the mind stops exploring alternative interpretations. Repetition of language creates stability, but it can also create rigidity.

Social environments amplify repetition dramatically. Beliefs expressed by family, peers, media, and institutions are reinforced through constant exposure. Agreement signals safety and belonging, while deviation invites discomfort. As a result, repeated social narratives become internalized beliefs. The mind adopts group interpretations not because they are examined, but because they are reinforced. Over time, social repetition feels indistinguishable from personal conviction.

Repetition also shapes attention. What the mind repeatedly focuses on becomes more noticeable. Concerns that are revisited frequently occupy disproportionate mental space, even when they are statistically rare or objectively minor. Attention becomes trained, narrowing perception to familiar themes. This explains why individuals living in similar conditions can experience reality differently depending on what their minds habitually attend to.

Habitual thinking emerges from repetition without reflection. Once a mental process has been repeated enough times, it no longer requires conscious effort. Decisions are made quickly, judgments are formed instantly, and reactions feel intuitive. While this efficiency is useful, it reduces awareness. The mind operates on autopilot, repeating established patterns without reassessment. Thinking becomes predictable.

Importantly, repetition does not discriminate between helpful and harmful patterns. Productive reasoning and destructive rumination are reinforced through the same mechanism. A person who repeatedly questions assumptions strengthens analytical thinking, while one who repeatedly rehearses anxiety strengthens fear-based cognition. The brain treats both as skills to be optimized. Quality depends on content, not process.

Repetition also explains resistance to change. New ideas must compete with well-established neural patterns. Even accurate information feels uncomfortable if it conflicts with repeated beliefs. The mind experiences this discomfort as threat, triggering defensiveness. As a result, repetition protects existing mental structures regardless of their accuracy. Familiarity becomes a psychological shield.

Learning itself relies on repetition, but effective learning requires variation and reflection. Pure repetition without evaluation creates rote behavior rather than understanding. When repetition is combined with feedback, adjustment, and awareness, it produces flexible thinking. Without these elements, it produces rigidity. The difference lies not in repetition alone, but in how it is guided.

Modern technology accelerates mental repetition at unprecedented speed. Algorithms deliver repeated content aligned with prior preferences, reinforcing beliefs and emotional responses continuously. Exposure becomes concentrated rather than diverse. The mind is trained through repetition without conscious consent. Over time, this environment shapes perception, attention, and belief formation in subtle but powerful ways.

Breaking the influence of repetition requires intentional interruption. Awareness introduces friction into automatic processes. By noticing repeated thoughts, questioning their origin, and examining their accuracy, individuals weaken their dominance. New repetition must then be established deliberately. The mind does not abandon habits through logic alone, but through replacement.

Ultimately, repetition is neither enemy nor ally. It is a neutral force that shapes mental processes according to exposure and practice. The mind becomes what it repeatedly does. Understanding this principle shifts responsibility from innate ability to daily mental behavior. What we think tomorrow depends largely on what we repeatedly think today.

Recognizing the role of repetition allows individuals to reclaim agency over their mental lives. By choosing what to expose the mind to, what narratives to rehearse, and what patterns to reinforce, thinking itself can be trained. The same mechanism that once shaped the mind unconsciously can be used consciously. Repetition, when directed, becomes the foundation of deliberate thinking.

Why Some Thoughts Feel Effortless

Some thoughts arrive in the mind with remarkable ease. They appear instantly, without hesitation, analysis, or conscious effort. Judgments form in seconds. Opinions feel obvious. Reactions seem natural. By contrast, other thoughts require struggle—deliberate focus, sustained attention, and mental energy. This difference is not random, nor is it a reflection of intelligence. It is the result of habit, repetition, and the brain's fundamental drive for efficiency.

The human brain is not designed to think deeply by default. Its primary function is survival, not truth-seeking or intellectual rigor. To survive, the brain must process information quickly, conserve energy, and respond predictably to familiar situations. Thoughts that feel effortless are those that align with these goals. They are thoughts the brain has practiced repeatedly, optimized over time, and automated for speed.

Effortless thoughts are habits. They have been rehearsed so often that they no longer require conscious control. Each repetition strengthens the neural pathways associated with that thought, making activation faster and more reliable. Over time, the brain learns that this particular pattern "works" in the sense that it resolves uncertainty quickly and reduces cognitive strain. Accuracy becomes secondary to efficiency.

This is why familiar interpretations feel correct even before they are examined. When a situation resembles a past experience, the brain retrieves an established response automatically. The mind does not ask whether the response is appropriate or accurate; it asks whether it is familiar. Familiarity signals safety. The thought feels smooth, intuitive, and unquestionable because it does not encounter resistance within the mental system.

Effortless thoughts are often mistaken for insight. Because they arise quickly and confidently, they feel intelligent. In reality, speed reflects conditioning, not depth. A thought that has been repeated thousands of times will surface faster than a thought that requires new analysis, regardless of its quality. This creates a dangerous illusion: the mind equates ease with correctness.

Emotion plays a crucial role in this process. Thoughts linked to strong emotions are reinforced more aggressively. Fear, pleasure, anger, and shame imprint patterns deeply into memory. Each emotional replay strengthens the association between stimulus and response. Over time, similar situations trigger the same thought automatically, bypassing conscious evaluation. The emotional brain signals urgency, and the cognitive brain complies.

Language further accelerates effortless thinking. Words provide shortcuts that compress complex realities into simple categories. Repeated phrases, labels, and narratives become mental templates. Once something is labeled, the mind stops analyzing it. The label feels sufficient. Repetition of language trains the brain to respond to words rather than evidence. The thought feels effortless because the work has already been outsourced to habit.

Social reinforcement intensifies this effect. Thoughts shared and validated by others are repeated more often and with greater confidence. Agreement reduces uncertainty and strengthens belief. Over time, socially reinforced thoughts feel natural and self-generated, even when they originated externally. The mind internalizes repetition as personal conviction.

Attention also determines effortlessness. What the mind attends to repeatedly becomes easier to notice and interpret. Patterns emerge not because they are objectively dominant, but because attention has been trained to detect them. This selective attention makes certain thoughts feel obvious while others remain invisible. The mind sees what it has learned to see.

Cognitive shortcuts, often called heuristics, are another source of effortless thought. These shortcuts allow the brain to make rapid judgments using minimal information. While useful in many situations, they rely on generalization rather than analysis. Once a shortcut is learned and reinforced, it becomes automatic. The thought feels effortless because the brain bypasses evaluation entirely.

Importantly, effortless thinking is not inherently negative. It allows humans to function efficiently in complex environments. Driving, speaking, reading, and basic social interaction all rely on automated thinking. Without it, daily life would be exhausting. The problem arises when effortless thinking dominates areas that require reflection, judgment, and adaptation.

When the mind relies too heavily on effortless thoughts, it becomes rigid. New information is filtered through existing patterns rather than assessed on its own merits. Contradictions are dismissed instinctively. The mind experiences discomfort when confronted with unfamiliar ideas because they require effort. That discomfort is often misinterpreted as evidence that the idea is wrong.

This resistance is not intellectual; it is neurological. Effortful thinking requires the brain to slow down, allocate energy, and tolerate uncertainty. The brain perceives this as inefficient and mildly threatening. Effortless thoughts, by contrast, restore equilibrium quickly. They close questions instead of opening them.

Over time, people begin to identify with their effortless thoughts. Because these thoughts arise automatically, they feel like expressions of the self. Challenging them feels personal. The mind defends them not because they are accurate, but because they are familiar. Habit masquerades as identity.

Effortless thinking also explains why change is difficult even when people recognize the need for it. Awareness alone does not dissolve habits. The brain continues to default to well-worn pathways unless new ones are deliberately practiced. Logical understanding competes with years of repetition. Without replacement, old patterns persist.

The modern environment amplifies effortless thinking dramatically. Constant exposure to repeated messages trains the mind continuously. Algorithms prioritize familiarity, reinforcing existing preferences and beliefs. The brain is rewarded with ease and comfort, while effortful thinking is discouraged through overload and distraction. As a result, effortless thoughts become dominant not by choice, but by design.

Effortless thoughts are also closely linked to confidence. Because they arise without hesitation, they feel certain. This confidence can be persuasive, both internally and socially. However, confidence does not correlate with accuracy. The mind often confuses the absence of effort with the presence of truth.

Developing better thinking does not mean eliminating effortless thoughts, but recognizing their limitations. Effortless thoughts are efficient responses to familiar situations, not guarantees of correctness. Mature thinking involves knowing when to rely on habit and when to intervene with reflection.

Effortful thinking begins with awareness. Noticing which thoughts arrive automatically creates distance. Questioning their origin, emotional charge, and assumptions introduces friction into the process. This friction slows the mind down, allowing alternative interpretations to emerge. Over time, new patterns can be practiced until they too become effortless.

This is the paradox of thinking: what feels effortless was once effortful. Every automatic skill began as deliberate practice. The quality of effortless thinking depends entirely on what has been repeated. If poor reasoning is rehearsed, poor reasoning becomes easy. If reflective thinking is practiced, reflection becomes natural.

Ultimately, some thoughts feel effortless because the brain has been trained to produce them efficiently. They are not signs of intelligence, insight, or truth. They are signs of repetition. Understanding this restores agency. The mind is not bound by what feels easy; it is shaped by what it practices. By choosing what thoughts to repeat, individuals determine which thoughts will one day feel effortless—and which will no longer control them.

The Myth of "Natural Thinkers"

The idea of the "natural thinker" is deeply embedded in modern culture. From classrooms to workplaces, certain individuals are praised as being inherently analytical, logical, or insightful, while others are quietly categorized as less capable of deep thought. This belief suggests that thinking well is a gift—something bestowed at birth rather than developed through effort. Although appealing in its simplicity, this narrative is misleading. It obscures how thinking actually develops and discourages many people from engaging fully with their intellectual potential. The so-called natural thinker is not born; they are trained, conditioned, and shaped by repeated mental practice.

The myth persists because thinking skill often appears effortless in those who have practiced it extensively. When someone articulates ideas clearly, identifies patterns quickly, or asks sharp questions, observers assume innate ability. What is invisible is the accumulation of experiences that made such thinking automatic. Years of reading, questioning, exposure to feedback, failure, and refinement are compressed into a moment of apparent ease. Habit masquerades as talent.

This misconception begins early. In educational settings, children who grasp concepts quickly are labeled "smart," while others are labeled "average" or "weak." Rarely is attention paid to how these children are thinking, what strategies they use, or what prior exposure they have had. The label becomes a self-fulfilling prophecy. Those praised for being natural thinkers are encouraged to continue engaging, while others disengage, believing effort will not change their standing. In reality, both groups are responding to reinforcement, not destiny.

Thinking is not a single ability; it is a collection of skills. These include attention control, pattern recognition, abstraction, evaluation, perspective-taking, and self-correction. Each of these skills can be practiced, strengthened, or neglected. No one is born fluent in these processes. They are learned through repetition in environments that reward curiosity and reflection. When these environments are absent, even highly intelligent individuals may never develop strong thinking habits.

The myth of natural thinkers also ignores the role of privilege and exposure. Individuals raised in environments rich in language, discussion, and intellectual challenge are more likely to develop advanced thinking patterns early. This advantage is often mistaken for innate brilliance. Meanwhile, those raised in environments focused on survival, obedience, or rote instruction may not have the opportunity to practice reflective thinking. The difference is environmental, not biological.

Another reason the myth persists is that thinking habits are domain-specific. A person may demonstrate exceptional thinking in one area and struggle in another. A scientist may reason rigorously in the lab yet rely on unexamined beliefs in social or political matters. This inconsistency contradicts the idea of a generalized natural thinker. It supports the reality that thinking develops where it is practiced and withers where it is not.

The belief in natural thinkers also serves a psychological function. It absolves institutions of responsibility. If thinking ability is innate, then educational systems are not obligated to teach thinking explicitly. They can focus on content delivery and assessment rather than skill development. Failure is attributed to the individual rather than the method. This perspective benefits systems but harms learners.

Social narratives reinforce the myth through selective storytelling. Biographies of famous intellectuals often highlight moments of brilliance while minimizing years of struggle, revision, and uncertainty. Breakthroughs are portrayed as flashes of insight rather than the culmination of sustained effort. This distorts expectations and reinforces the illusion that great thinking emerges spontaneously.

The myth also affects those labeled as natural thinkers. When individuals internalize this identity, they may avoid challenges that threaten it. Effort becomes risky; struggle becomes evidence of inadequacy. As a result, growth stagnates. Those who believe their value lies in effortless performance may resist learning opportunities that require sustained effort. Ironically, the belief in natural thinking can undermine actual thinking development.

In contrast, individuals who view thinking as a skill are more resilient. They expect difficulty, welcome feedback, and persist through confusion. Their progress may be slower initially, but it is more durable. Over time, their thinking becomes refined and flexible. What once required effort begins to feel natural—not because it always was, but because it has been practiced.

The myth of natural thinkers also distorts how society evaluates ideas. Confident delivery is often mistaken for sound reasoning. Individuals who speak fluently and assertively are assumed to be better thinkers, even when their arguments lack evidence or coherence. Meanwhile, those who think carefully but speak cautiously may be overlooked. This preference for style over substance rewards performance rather than reasoning.

Emotion further complicates the myth. People often equate calmness and confidence with rationality. In reality, emotional regulation is a learned skill. Those who appear composed under pressure have practiced managing cognitive load and uncertainty. Their calm is not innate; it is conditioned. Without recognizing this, others may assume they lack the capacity for similar composure.

The myth also intersects with cultural bias. Certain ways of speaking, reasoning, and expressing ideas are valued over others. Individuals who align with dominant norms are more likely to be labeled natural thinkers. This marginalizes alternative cognitive styles and reinforces inequality. Thinking ability is judged through narrow lenses rather than genuine evaluation of reasoning quality.

Scientific research consistently challenges the idea of fixed thinking ability. Neuroplasticity demonstrates that the brain changes in response to experience throughout life. New neural connections form with practice; unused pathways weaken. Thinking patterns are not static traits but dynamic processes. The brain becomes what it repeatedly does. This applies as much to reasoning as it does to motor skills.

Understanding thinking as a habit rather than a gift has profound implications. It democratizes intellectual growth. Everyone becomes capable of improvement, regardless of starting point. The question shifts from "Who is a natural thinker?" to "What thinking habits are being practiced?" This shift empowers individuals and holds systems accountable.

The myth of natural thinkers persists because it is simple, flattering to some, and convenient for many. But it is inaccurate and limiting. It discourages effort, masks inequality, and misrepresents how the mind works. Thinking is not a rare talent possessed by a few. It is a skill cultivated by many, through repetition, feedback, and deliberate practice.

Ultimately, the most effective thinkers are not those born with special minds, but those who have spent time training their thinking. Their apparent ease is the product of discipline, not destiny. By abandoning the myth of natural thinkers, we reclaim the possibility of intellectual growth for everyone. The mind is not defined by what it is given, but by what it repeatedly practices.

Chapter 2

How the Mind Learns Patterns

The human mind is a pattern-detecting system long before it is a reasoning one. From the earliest moments of life, the brain organizes experience by identifying regularities—what tends to happen next, which signals predict reward or threat, and how actions lead to outcomes. This capacity allows human beings to navigate a complex world efficiently. Yet the same mechanism that enables learning also shapes perception, belief, and behavior in ways that often operate beneath awareness.

Patterns are not learned through logic at first; they are learned through exposure. Repetition teaches the mind what to expect. When events, reactions, or ideas recur in similar forms, the brain links them together, forming predictive models of reality. These models are not neutral descriptions of the world; they are practical shortcuts designed to reduce uncertainty. Once a pattern is established, the mind begins to treat it as a rule.

This is why the mind often responds to situations before conscious thought has time to intervene. The brain recognizes a familiar configuration of cues—tone of voice, facial expression, context, or language—and activates an associated response automatically. In many cases, this is useful. It allows rapid decision-making and efficient action. However, it also means that interpretation precedes evaluation. The mind does not ask whether a pattern is accurate; it asks whether it is familiar.

Patterns are reinforced not only by frequency, but by emotional relevance. Experiences paired with strong emotion—fear, pleasure, shame, approval—are encoded more deeply and recalled more readily. Each emotional replay strengthens the associated pattern, increasing the likelihood that it will be activated again. Over time, the mind becomes biased toward patterns that carry emotional weight, regardless of their factual reliability.

Language accelerates this process. Words create categories, and categories create patterns. Once an experience is named, it becomes easier to recognize—and harder to reinterpret. Repeated language shapes how situations are perceived, which aspects are emphasized, and which are ignored. Patterns formed through language feel especially solid because they provide narrative coherence. The mind prefers stories that repeat to explanations that evolve.

Social environments further intensify pattern learning. Beliefs modeled by caregivers, peers, institutions, and media are reinforced through constant exposure. Agreement signals safety and belonging, while deviation introduces discomfort. As a result, social patterns are often internalized without examination. The mind absorbs shared interpretations and treats them as personal insight. Over time, social repetition becomes cognitive certainty.

Importantly, the mind does not distinguish between accurate and inaccurate patterns during learning. It strengthens whatever is repeated and rewarded. Helpful reasoning and harmful bias are reinforced by the same neurological process. If an assumption consistently reduces discomfort or gains approval, it is likely to be repeated—even if it distorts reality. Pattern learning optimizes for predictability, not truth.

This explains why the mind often resists new information. New data must compete with established patterns that already feel stable and reliable. When information conflicts with an existing pattern, it creates cognitive tension. Rather than revising the pattern, the mind often rejects or reinterprets the information. Familiarity functions as a filter, shaping what is noticed, believed, and remembered.

Pattern learning also influences attention. The mind becomes skilled at noticing what fits established models and overlooking what does not. Over time, perception narrows. The world appears consistent not because it is simple, but because the mind has learned which elements to emphasize. This selective attention reinforces patterns further, creating a self-sustaining loop.

Understanding how the mind learns patterns is essential for understanding thinking itself. Thought is not a blank-slate process applied anew to each situation; it is the activation of learned structures. These structures guide interpretation long before deliberate reasoning begins. Without awareness, thinking becomes repetition.

This chapter explores the mechanisms through which patterns are formed, reinforced, and maintained. By examining the roles of repetition, emotion, language, and social influence, we begin to see how the mind constructs its version of reality. Recognizing these processes does not eliminate pattern learning—nor should it. Instead, it allows us to distinguish between patterns that serve understanding and those that merely preserve familiarity.

To think well, one must first understand how thinking has been trained. Pattern awareness is the foundation of mental freedom.

Neural Pathways and Repeated Thought Loops

The human brain is not a static organ but a living network of connections that constantly reorganizes itself in response to experience. At the core of this adaptability lies the formation and reinforcement of neural pathways. Every thought, perception, emotion, and action corresponds to patterns of neural activity. When these patterns repeat, the brain changes. Pathways strengthen, signals travel faster, and mental processes become increasingly automatic. This is the biological foundation of repeated thought loops.

A neural pathway is a chain of neurons that communicate through electrical and chemical signals. When a particular set of neurons activates together, the connection between them becomes more efficient. This process, often summarized as "neurons that fire together wire together," explains how repetition shapes mental life. The brain does not store thoughts as isolated ideas; it stores patterns of activation. The more often a pattern is activated, the more easily it is triggered again.

Repeated thought loops form when the same mental pattern is activated over and over, often without conscious intention. These loops can involve beliefs, worries, interpretations, memories, or expectations. Once established, they operate with minimal effort. The brain treats them as reliable shortcuts, preferring them over unfamiliar or effortful alternatives. This preference is not a matter of choice; it is a matter of neural efficiency.

The brain's drive for efficiency is central to understanding repeated thought loops. Conscious, analytical thinking requires significant energy. It involves sustained attention, working memory, and executive control. Repeated patterns reduce this cost. When a familiar thought loop is activated, the brain conserves energy by bypassing evaluation and reflection. The loop resolves uncertainty quickly, restoring a sense of cognitive stability.

Early experiences play a critical role in shaping these pathways. During childhood, the brain is especially plastic. Neural connections form rapidly in response to repeated interactions, emotional responses, and environmental cues. Interpretations learned early are often reinforced over time, not because they are accurate, but because they are repeatedly reactivated. These early pathways become default modes of perception in adulthood.

Emotion strongly influences which pathways are reinforced. Emotional arousal increases neural activation, making associated pathways more likely to strengthen. Fear-based thoughts, for example, are rehearsed frequently because they are triggered by perceived threat. Each rehearsal deepens the pathway, making the fear response faster and more automatic. Over time, the loop activates even in situations that only loosely resemble the original trigger.

Memory contributes to this process by replaying past experiences. Remembering is not a passive retrieval of stored information; it is an active reconstruction that reactivates neural pathways. Each recall strengthens the associated network. This is why certain memories feel vivid and persistent. They have been replayed repeatedly, reinforcing both the content of the memory and the emotional response attached to it.

Language further stabilizes thought loops. Words provide structure to neural activity by linking concepts together. Repeated phrases, narratives, and self-descriptions become embedded in neural circuits. Internal dialogue rehearses these circuits continuously. Over time, language-based thought loops shape identity itself. The brain learns not only what to think, but how to think about the self.

Social reinforcement accelerates the formation of repeated loops. Agreement from others strengthens confidence in a thought, increasing the likelihood of repetition. Disagreement, by contrast, often triggers defensiveness, which paradoxically reinforces the original loop. The brain prioritizes social stability, so thoughts that maintain belonging are rehearsed more frequently. Neural pathways align with social patterns as much as with personal experience.

Once established, thought loops become self-sustaining. Selective attention reinforces them by focusing perception on information that fits the existing pattern. Contradictory information is filtered out or reinterpreted. This creates a feedback loop in which the brain repeatedly confirms its own expectations. The pathway grows stronger not because it is challenged, but because it is protected.

Importantly, the brain does not distinguish between constructive and destructive loops. Productive reasoning and harmful rumination rely on the same mechanisms. A person who repeatedly analyzes problems develops efficient analytical pathways. A person who repeatedly worries develops efficient anxiety pathways. The brain optimizes whatever is practiced most frequently. Quality is irrelevant to the wiring process.

Repeated thought loops also explain why change feels difficult even when it is desired. New ways of thinking require the formation of new pathways, which initially feel slow and effortful. Existing pathways resist deactivation because they are efficient and familiar. The brain interprets this effort as discomfort. As a result, individuals often revert to old loops despite conscious intentions to change.

Stress intensifies reliance on established pathways. Under pressure, the brain prioritizes speed over flexibility. Executive functions weaken, and habitual responses dominate. This is why people often repeat the same patterns during conflict, anxiety, or fatigue. Stress does not create new thinking; it reveals what has already been wired through repetition.

Modern environments amplify repeated thought loops dramatically. Constant exposure to similar information reinforces specific neural pathways continuously. Digital platforms repeat content aligned with existing preferences, strengthening belief loops without reflection. The brain adapts quickly, optimizing for familiarity. Over time, this reduces cognitive diversity and increases rigidity.

However, neural pathways are not permanent. Neuroplasticity persists throughout life. Pathways weaken when they are no longer activated, and new ones form with practice. This means that repeated thought loops can be altered, but not through insight alone. Change requires repetition. New patterns must be activated consistently to compete with established ones.

Awareness is the first step in disrupting loops. Noticing a repeated thought introduces a pause in automatic activation. This pause engages higher-order brain regions involved in monitoring and control. While awareness alone does not rewire the brain, it creates the conditions for change by interrupting automaticity.

Deliberate practice is essential. Replacing a thought loop requires repeated engagement with an alternative pattern. This may involve questioning assumptions, reframing interpretations, or redirecting attention. Each repetition strengthens the new pathway incrementally. Over time, what was once effortful becomes easier, and the old loop weakens through disuse.

Emotional regulation supports this process by reducing the intensity that reinforces old loops. When emotional arousal decreases, neural activation becomes less rigid. This creates flexibility, allowing new pathways to form. Calm states are more conducive to cognitive change than reactive ones.

Understanding neural pathways and repeated thought loops shifts responsibility from identity to practice. Thoughts feel personal, but they are biological patterns shaped by repetition. The brain does not cling to ideas because they define the self; it clings to them because they are efficient. Recognizing this reduces self-blame and increases agency.

Ultimately, repeated thought loops are the physical expression of mental habit. They explain why thinking feels automatic, why beliefs persist, and why change requires effort. The mind is not fixed by nature; it is shaped by what it repeatedly activates. By understanding how neural pathways form and function, individuals gain the ability to train their thinking intentionally. What the brain practices, it becomes.

Learning Through Exposure and Reinforcement

Learning does not begin with instruction, explanation, or conscious intention. It begins with exposure. Long before the mind can analyze or reflect, it absorbs patterns simply by encountering them repeatedly. Sounds, behaviors, emotional reactions, social norms, and interpretations are learned not because they are evaluated, but because they are present. Exposure lays the foundation of learning, and reinforcement determines which elements of that exposure endure.

Exposure is the process by which the mind becomes familiar with stimuli. Reinforcement is the mechanism that signals which of those stimuli should be repeated, remembered, or prioritized. Together, they form the primary engine of mental development. What the mind encounters most often—and what produces reward, relief, or approval—becomes ingrained. This process operates continuously, shaping thoughts, beliefs, habits, and identity itself.

The brain is designed to learn through exposure because repetition reduces uncertainty. Familiarity allows prediction, and prediction supports survival. When the same pattern appears repeatedly, the brain treats it as reliable. Neural resources are allocated accordingly, strengthening pathways associated with that pattern. Over time, the pattern becomes automatic, no longer requiring conscious attention. Learning has occurred, even if no deliberate effort was made.

Reinforcement determines direction. Not all exposure leads to lasting learning. The brain selectively strengthens patterns that are reinforced—either positively or negatively. Positive reinforcement includes rewards such as pleasure, praise, relief, or success. Negative reinforcement involves the removal of discomfort, fear, or uncertainty. Both signal to the brain that a particular response is effective and should be repeated.

This is why learning is not inherently aligned with truth or accuracy. The brain does not reinforce what is correct; it reinforces what works in reducing discomfort or increasing reward. A belief that lowers anxiety, even if inaccurate, may be reinforced more strongly than a belief that introduces uncertainty. Over time, the mind becomes skilled at maintaining comfort rather than pursuing accuracy.

Early learning demonstrates this clearly. Children learn emotional responses by observing and repeating those of caregivers. If certain reactions consistently result in approval or attention, they are reinforced. If others result in punishment or withdrawal, they are suppressed. The child does not analyze these outcomes; the brain simply learns which patterns are rewarded. These learned responses often persist into adulthood, long after the original context has disappeared.

Language learning offers another clear example. Words and meanings are acquired through repeated exposure and reinforcement, not through formal explanation alone. The mind associates sounds with outcomes. When a word produces understanding, connection, or response, it is reinforced. Over time, language becomes automatic. This same mechanism applies to internal language—the narratives individuals repeat about themselves and the world.

Social environments are powerful sources of reinforcement. Agreement, belonging, and acceptance function as strong rewards. When certain beliefs or interpretations align with group norms, they are reinforced through validation. When they deviate, discomfort follows. As a result, exposure to repeated social narratives shapes belief systems deeply. The mind learns not only what is common, but what is safe to think.

Reinforcement also explains why misinformation can be learned as easily as accurate information. If repeated exposure is paired with emotional engagement or social approval, the brain strengthens the associated pathways. Familiarity becomes indistinguishable from credibility. The mind feels confident not because it has evaluated evidence, but because it has been reinforced repeatedly.

Learning through exposure is not limited to external input. Internal experiences are also reinforced. Thoughts that reduce distress, justify decisions, or protect self-image are rehearsed frequently. Each rehearsal strengthens the pattern. Over time, internal narratives become stable mental habits. The mind learns how to interpret events based on what has previously restored equilibrium.

Importantly, reinforcement does not require conscious awareness. Many learned patterns operate below the level of reflection. People often cannot explain why they think or react the way they do because the learning occurred implicitly. The brain learned through outcomes, not reasoning. This implicit learning is efficient, but it is also resistant to change.

The educational implications of this process are profound. Instruction alone is insufficient if reinforcement contradicts it. A learner may be taught critical thinking, but if speed and correctness are rewarded instead of reflection and questioning, superficial habits will dominate. Reinforcement determines which skills are practiced and retained. Learning follows reward, not intention.

Reinforcement also shapes attention. What the mind is rewarded for noticing becomes more noticeable. If certain cues consistently predict reward or threat, attention becomes trained to detect them. Over time, perception itself changes. The world appears structured according to learned priorities. This selective perception reinforces existing patterns, creating self-sustaining loops.

Negative reinforcement is especially influential. Avoiding discomfort can be a stronger motivator than seeking reward. Thoughts or behaviors that reduce anxiety, even temporarily, are likely to be repeated. This explains the persistence of avoidance, denial, and rationalization. The mind learns to repeat whatever restores comfort quickly, regardless of long-term consequences.

Change requires disrupting reinforcement patterns. New learning does not occur simply by introducing new information. It occurs when reinforcement shifts. When effortful thinking is rewarded, it increases. When automatic reactions are no longer reinforced, they weaken. Without this shift, exposure alone is insufficient to alter behavior or belief.

Modern environments intensify exposure and reinforcement simultaneously. Repeated content is delivered alongside emotional engagement, social validation, and algorithmic reward. The brain is trained continuously, often without awareness. This environment favors repetition over reflection, familiarity over accuracy. Learning occurs rapidly, but not always wisely.

However, the same mechanisms that shape unexamined thinking can be used deliberately. By controlling exposure and redefining reinforcement, individuals can retrain their minds. Repeated engagement with challenging ideas, paired with satisfaction from understanding rather than comfort from certainty, builds stronger thinking habits. Reflection becomes rewarding through practice.

Learning through exposure and reinforcement reveals that the mind is not guided primarily by logic, but by experience. Beliefs, preferences, and interpretations are shaped by what has been encountered most often and reinforced most consistently. Understanding this process restores agency. It allows individuals to examine not only what they think, but why they think it.

Ultimately, learning is not a one-time event but an ongoing process of pattern strengthening. The mind becomes what it repeatedly experiences and rewards. By becoming conscious of exposure and reinforcement, thinking itself can be trained intentionally. What is reinforced today becomes habitual tomorrow.

Why Familiar Ideas Feel "True"

Human beings rarely experience truth as a conclusion reached through careful analysis. More often, truth is felt. Certain ideas register immediately as obvious, reasonable, or beyond question, while others provoke resistance or discomfort before they are even examined. This intuitive sense of truth is not a reliable indicator of accuracy. It is, instead, a psychological response shaped by familiarity. Ideas feel true not because they are correct, but because they are known.

The mind is structured to favor the familiar. Familiarity signals safety, predictability, and coherence. When an idea has been encountered repeatedly—through language, culture, education, or personal experience—the brain processes it with ease. This ease is experienced subjectively as confidence. The thought feels smooth, unchallenged, and stable. In contrast, unfamiliar ideas require effort. They slow the mind down, introduce uncertainty, and disrupt existing mental structures. The discomfort that accompanies this effort is often mistaken for evidence that the idea is flawed.

This phenomenon is rooted in cognitive fluency. Cognitive fluency refers to the ease with which information is processed. Information that is processed fluently feels more convincing, more trustworthy, and more accurate than information that is processed with difficulty. Repetition increases fluency. Each exposure reduces the mental effort required to recognize and interpret an idea. Over time, fluency becomes indistinguishable from truth in subjective experience.

The brain interprets fluency as reliability because, from an evolutionary perspective, familiar patterns were less likely to be dangerous. If something had been encountered repeatedly without harm, it was probably safe. This survival mechanism, while useful in physical environments, becomes misleading in abstract domains such as beliefs, opinions, and interpretations. The mind applies the same logic to ideas that it applies to objects: what is familiar is assumed to be trustworthy.

Memory reinforces this effect. Each time an idea is recalled, it is reactivated and strengthened. Recall does not simply retrieve information; it reconstructs it, reinforcing associated emotions and interpretations. An idea that is frequently remembered feels established and stable. The mind confuses stability with validity. Over time, the repeated memory of an idea creates the impression that it has always been known, further reinforcing its perceived truth.

Emotion amplifies familiarity's influence. Ideas associated with emotional comfort, identity, or belonging are rehearsed more frequently. Each rehearsal strengthens both the idea and the emotional response attached to it. This creates a powerful bond between familiarity and emotional security. Challenging such ideas feels threatening not because the ideas are accurate, but because they are emotionally reinforced. The mind defends them to preserve equilibrium.

Language plays a critical role in making familiar ideas feel true. Words shape thought by providing ready-made frameworks for interpretation. Repeated phrases, slogans, and narratives simplify complex realities into digestible forms. Once internalized, these linguistic patterns guide perception automatically. The idea feels true because it fits a known narrative structure. The mind prefers coherence over accuracy, and familiar language provides coherence effortlessly.

Social reinforcement intensifies this effect. Ideas shared by groups are repeated, validated, and echoed across interactions. Agreement from others signals correctness. Over time, the mind internalizes socially reinforced ideas as personal convictions. The boundary between belief and belonging dissolves. Familiar group ideas feel true because rejecting them risks social discomfort. Truth becomes associated with acceptance rather than evidence.

The illusion of truth effect further explains this phenomenon. Psychological research consistently shows that repeated statements are more likely to be judged as true, regardless of their factual accuracy. Repetition alone increases perceived credibility. The mind does not ask whether an idea has been proven; it registers that it has been heard before. Familiarity becomes a substitute for verification.

This mechanism also explains why misinformation spreads so effectively. Repeated exposure creates familiarity, which creates perceived truth. Even when people know an idea may be false, repeated encounters can still increase its believability. The rational mind may object, but the intuitive mind responds to fluency. The feeling of truth arises before analysis can intervene.

Familiar ideas also align with existing mental patterns. The mind organizes information into schemas—structured frameworks that guide interpretation. New ideas that fit existing schemas are processed easily and accepted readily. Ideas that challenge schemas require reorganization, which is effortful and uncomfortable. The mind prefers confirmation to revision. Familiar ideas feel true because they reinforce what is already believed.

Confidence further strengthens this illusion. Familiar ideas are often expressed with certainty because they require little effort to articulate. This confidence is persuasive, both internally and externally. The mind interprets confident expression as evidence of truth. In reality, confidence often reflects repetition, not correctness. Ideas repeated frequently are expressed fluently, and fluency is mistaken for authority.

Time also plays a role. Ideas learned early feel especially true because they have been reinforced for longer periods. Early beliefs become reference points against which new information is judged. The longer an idea has been familiar, the more entrenched it feels. Longevity creates legitimacy in subjective experience, even when the idea has never been critically examined.

The mind's resistance to unfamiliar ideas is not a sign of poor intelligence; it is a feature of cognitive efficiency. However, this feature becomes a limitation when familiarity replaces evaluation. Truth becomes defined by comfort rather than correspondence with reality. Thinking becomes repetitive rather than reflective.

Understanding why familiar ideas feel true is essential for developing intellectual humility. It reveals that certainty is often a feeling, not a conclusion. The feeling of truth arises from exposure, repetition, and reinforcement, not from careful reasoning alone. Recognizing this does not mean rejecting familiar ideas automatically; it means suspending judgment until evaluation occurs.

Critical thinking requires tolerance for discomfort. New ideas should feel effortful if they are genuinely new. Discomfort is not evidence of falsehood; it is evidence of cognitive work. When the mind learns to separate familiarity from truth, it becomes capable of growth.

Ultimately, ideas feel true because the mind is trained to trust what it knows. Familiarity reduces effort, uncertainty, and emotional strain. But truth demands more than comfort. It demands examination. By understanding the psychological forces that make familiarity feel like truth, individuals gain the ability to question certainty without fear. The mind becomes less governed by repetition and more guided by reason.

Pattern Recognition vs. Critical Reasoning

The human mind relies on two fundamentally different modes of cognition to navigate the world: pattern recognition and critical reasoning. Both are essential, both are powerful, and both shape how individuals perceive reality, make decisions, and form beliefs. However, these two modes operate in profoundly different ways and often produce very different outcomes. Confusing pattern recognition with critical reasoning is one of the most common—and consequential—errors in human thinking.

Pattern recognition is the brain's ability to identify regularities in experience. It allows the mind to notice similarities, predict outcomes, and respond quickly to familiar situations. This capacity develops early and operates largely outside conscious awareness. Critical reasoning, by contrast, is deliberate, reflective, and evaluative. It involves questioning assumptions, examining evidence, comparing alternatives, and revising conclusions when necessary. While pattern recognition prioritizes speed and efficiency, critical reasoning prioritizes accuracy and understanding.

Pattern recognition is automatic. The brain continuously scans the environment for cues it has seen before. When a familiar configuration appears, the associated response is activated instantly. This process requires little energy and minimal attention. It is the reason humans can recognize faces, understand language, and navigate social situations effortlessly. Without pattern recognition, everyday life would be cognitively overwhelming.

However, pattern recognition does not ask whether a pattern is valid; it only asks whether it is familiar. The brain treats repetition as reliability. When a pattern has appeared frequently in the past, the mind assumes it will apply again in the future. This assumption is often useful, but it is also deeply flawed. Many patterns persist not because they are accurate, but because they have been reinforced through repetition, emotion, or social validation.

Critical reasoning operates differently. It interrupts automatic responses and introduces evaluation. Instead of asking, "Have I seen this before?" it asks, "What is actually happening here?" This mode of thinking requires conscious effort. It draws on attention, working memory, and self-regulation. Critical reasoning is slower because it resists immediate closure. It tolerates uncertainty in order to reach better conclusions.

The key difference between these modes lies in their relationship to familiarity. Pattern recognition thrives on familiarity; critical reasoning challenges it. When a situation fits an existing pattern, pattern recognition feels comfortable and confident. Critical reasoning, however, becomes most necessary precisely when familiarity is misleading—when a situation looks similar to past experiences but differs in important ways. In such moments, reliance on pattern recognition leads to error.

Pattern recognition excels in stable environments where conditions repeat reliably. It allows rapid decision-making without constant analysis. Critical reasoning becomes essential in complex, ambiguous, or novel situations where surface similarities mask deeper differences. The danger arises when pattern recognition dominates contexts that require reasoning. The mind mistakes resemblance for equivalence and speed for insight.

Emotion strongly biases pattern recognition. Emotional experiences are encoded deeply and replayed frequently, making associated patterns more accessible. When an emotional cue appears, the brain activates the corresponding pattern instantly. Critical reasoning is often bypassed entirely. This is why emotionally charged topics provoke strong opinions that feel obvious and unquestionable. The mind is responding to learned patterns, not evaluated arguments.

Language further reinforces this dynamic. Repeated phrases and narratives become cognitive shortcuts. Once an idea fits a familiar linguistic pattern, it is accepted quickly. Critical reasoning requires unpacking these narratives, examining their assumptions, and testing their coherence. This process feels effortful and disruptive. As a result, the mind often defaults to pattern recognition disguised as reasoning.

Social environments amplify reliance on pattern recognition. Shared beliefs become reinforced through repetition and agreement. Group narratives form powerful patterns that shape perception. When many people express the same view, the mind interprets consensus as evidence. Critical reasoning, which might question the underlying logic or evidence, feels socially risky. Pattern recognition aligns with belonging; reasoning risks isolation.

Pattern recognition also explains why stereotypes are so persistent. They are learned patterns that simplify complex social realities. Once formed, they are reinforced selectively. Instances that confirm the pattern are noticed and remembered, while contradictory examples are overlooked. Critical reasoning would require examining the pattern itself—its origins, limitations, and inaccuracies. This examination is effortful and uncomfortable, so the pattern remains intact.

Critical reasoning depends on meta-cognition: the ability to think about one's own thinking. Pattern recognition lacks this capacity. It operates invisibly, producing conclusions without revealing its process. Critical reasoning, by contrast, makes reasoning explicit. It exposes assumptions, weighs alternatives, and remains open to revision. This transparency is its strength, but also its vulnerability. It invites doubt.

Speed is often mistaken for intelligence, which favors pattern recognition. Rapid responses appear confident and decisive. Critical reasoning appears slow and uncertain. In many cultures, decisiveness is valued over deliberation. As a result, pattern recognition is rewarded, while careful reasoning is undervalued. This preference leads to repeated errors that go unexamined because they feel familiar and efficient.

Importantly, pattern recognition is not flawed by nature. It is indispensable. The problem arises when it goes unchecked. Effective thinking involves knowing when to rely on patterns and when to question them. This requires awareness of context. Routine tasks benefit from pattern recognition. High-stakes decisions, ethical judgments, and novel problems demand critical reasoning.

The transition from pattern recognition to critical reasoning often begins with discomfort. When an automatic response does not fit the situation, tension arises. This tension is the signal that reasoning is needed. However, many people interpret discomfort as threat and retreat to familiar patterns. Critical reasoning requires the willingness to stay with discomfort long enough to examine it.

Education often fails to make this distinction explicit. Learners are taught to recognize patterns—formulas, procedures, expected answers—but are rarely taught to question them. As a result, pattern recognition is mistaken for understanding. Students may perform well without developing reasoning skills. When confronted with unfamiliar problems, they struggle because pattern recognition has no template to apply.

Critical reasoning develops through practice, not instruction alone. It requires repeated engagement with uncertainty, feedback, and error correction. Over time, reasoning itself can become habitual. The mind learns to pause, question, and evaluate automatically. In this way, critical reasoning can eventually feel more natural, though it never becomes as effortless as pattern recognition.

Modern information environments heavily favor pattern recognition. Algorithms deliver content aligned with existing beliefs, reinforcing familiar narratives. Exposure becomes repetitive, reducing the need for evaluation. The mind is trained to recognize and affirm patterns rather than to reason critically. This environment rewards agreement over analysis.

Understanding the difference between pattern recognition and critical reasoning restores intellectual agency. It clarifies why certainty feels compelling and why doubt feels uncomfortable. It reveals that many convictions are products of familiarity rather than evaluation. Recognizing this distinction does not eliminate pattern recognition; it places it in proper context.

Ultimately, pattern recognition answers the question, "What does this resemble?" Critical reasoning answers the question, "What is this, really?" Both are necessary. Wisdom lies in knowing which question to ask. When pattern recognition dominates, thinking becomes fast but shallow. When critical reasoning is engaged, thinking becomes slower but more accurate. The quality of thought depends not on eliminating patterns, but on subjecting them to reason.

Chapter 3

Memory: The Architect of Repetition

Memory is often understood as a storage system—a mental archive that preserves past experiences for later retrieval. While this description is partially accurate, it understates memory's true influence on thinking. Memory does not merely record what has happened; it actively shapes what happens next. It determines which thoughts return, which interpretations feel familiar, and which responses are activated automatically. In this sense, memory is not a passive container of the past, but the architect of repetition.

Every repeated thought begins with memory. When the mind encounters a situation, it does not assess it from a neutral starting point. Instead, it consults stored experiences, emotional associations, and learned interpretations. These memories provide ready-made frameworks that guide perception before conscious reasoning begins. What feels like an immediate understanding of the present is often the replay of the past.

Memory operates through reconstruction rather than replay. Each act of remembering reactivates neural pathways associated with an experience, reassembling it in the present moment. This reconstruction strengthens the pathway, making the same memory easier to access in the future. Over time, frequently recalled memories become dominant reference points, shaping expectations and interpretations. The mind learns not only what to remember, but how to think.

This process explains why certain thoughts recur persistently. Memories associated with emotion—especially fear, pleasure, shame, or reward—are recalled more often and with greater intensity. Each recall reinforces the emotional and cognitive pattern, increasing the likelihood that similar situations will trigger the same response. Memory, emotion, and repetition form a self-reinforcing loop.

Importantly, memory does not prioritize accuracy. It prioritizes coherence and relevance. Experiences that fit existing beliefs or emotional narratives are more likely to be recalled and rehearsed. Contradictory experiences fade or are reinterpreted to fit familiar patterns. Over time, memory becomes selective, reinforcing some interpretations while erasing others. The past becomes curated to support the present way of thinking.

Memory also influences identity. The stories individuals tell about themselves—who they are, what they can expect, and how the world works—are constructed from remembered experiences. These narratives are not fixed reflections of reality; they are assembled from repeated recall. Each repetition stabilizes the story, making it feel like an objective truth rather than a learned interpretation. Thinking becomes an extension of remembered identity.

Language plays a critical role in this process. Memories are often encoded and recalled through words. Repeated verbal descriptions shape how experiences are understood and remembered. Over time, language simplifies complex events into familiar narratives. The memory becomes less about what happened and more about how it has been described. Repetition of language reinforces repetition of thought.

Social reinforcement further strengthens memory-driven repetition. Shared memories are repeated in conversation, validated by others, and woven into collective narratives. Agreement strengthens recall. Disagreement introduces discomfort. As a result, socially reinforced memories become more vivid and influential. The mind learns which memories to rehearse and which to suppress based on social response.

Memory also trains attention. Experiences that have been remembered frequently become easier to notice again. The mind scans the environment for cues that resemble stored patterns. This selective attention increases the likelihood that familiar interpretations will be activated, reinforcing memory further. The cycle continues: memory shapes attention, attention shapes experience, and experience feeds memory.

Understanding memory as an active force rather than a passive record reveals why change is difficult. New ways of thinking must compete with deeply rehearsed memories that already guide perception. Even when individuals consciously reject a belief, memory-driven responses may persist. Insight alone cannot dismantle repetition; memory must be retrained through new experiences and repeated reinterpretation.

This chapter explores memory not as a backdrop to thinking, but as its engine. By examining how memories are formed, recalled, and reinforced, we begin to see how repetition becomes embedded in mental life. The mind repeats what memory preserves—and memory preserves what is rehearsed.

To change thinking, one must engage memory deliberately. Awareness of how the past shapes the present is the first step toward loosening repetition's grip. Memory may be the architect of repetition, but it is also a structure that can be redesigned.

How Experiences Are Stored in the Brain

Human experience does not enter the brain as a complete, unified record. Instead, it is broken down, distributed, and encoded across multiple systems that work together to create what we later call memory. Understanding how experiences are stored in the brain requires abandoning the idea of memory as a single container and replacing it with a more accurate model: memory as a dynamic network of associations shaped by perception, emotion, repetition, and meaning.

When an experience occurs, the brain does not store it as a literal snapshot of reality. Sensory systems first process different elements of the experience independently. Visual information is handled by visual regions, sounds by auditory regions, bodily sensations by somatosensory areas, and emotional responses by limbic structures. These components are processed simultaneously but separately. What we later recall as a single experience is actually a coordinated activation of many distributed neural systems.

The hippocampus plays a central role in organizing experiences into coherent memories. Rather than storing experiences itself, it acts as an index, binding together disparate elements—what happened, where it happened, when it happened, and how it felt. This binding allows the brain to reconstruct an experience later by reactivating the associated neural patterns. Without this coordination, experiences would remain fragmented and inaccessible to conscious recall.

Encoding is the first critical stage of memory storage. For an experience to be encoded, attention must be allocated to it. Experiences that pass unnoticed or are processed superficially leave weak or incomplete traces. Attention acts as a gatekeeper, determining which information is eligible for storage. This is why emotionally charged or novel experiences are remembered more clearly: they command attention and activate arousal systems that enhance encoding.

Emotion strongly influences how experiences are stored. The amygdala modulates memory formation by signaling the importance of an event. When an experience is emotionally significant, stress hormones and neurotransmitters enhance neural plasticity, strengthening the connections involved. This process increases the likelihood that the experience will be remembered and recalled later. The brain prioritizes experiences that may be relevant to future survival or well-being.

However, emotional enhancement does not guarantee accuracy. Emotional arousal strengthens memory consolidation, not fidelity. The brain stores the emotional meaning of an experience more reliably than its precise details. This is why people may remember how an event made them feel while misremembering what actually occurred. Emotional memory is adaptive, but it is not objective.

Once encoded, experiences undergo consolidation. Consolidation is the process by which initially fragile memory traces are stabilized over time. This process involves changes at the synaptic level, including the strengthening of neural connections through repeated activation. Sleep plays a critical role in consolidation. During certain sleep stages, the brain reactivates recent experiences, reinforcing relevant pathways and integrating new information with existing knowledge.

Consolidation is not a one-time event. Each time an experience is recalled, it enters a malleable state before being stored again. This process, known as reconsolidation, allows memories to be updated, modified, or distorted. New information, emotions, or interpretations introduced during recall can alter the memory itself. As a result, memory is not a static record of the past but a living construct that evolves with each retrieval.

The brain stores different types of experiences in different ways. Declarative memories, which include facts and events, rely heavily on the hippocampus and associated cortical areas. Procedural memories, such as skills and habits, are stored in networks involving the basal ganglia and cerebellum. Emotional associations are heavily influenced by the amygdala. These systems interact but operate according to distinct principles.

Procedural memory illustrates how experiences can be stored without conscious awareness. Skills such as walking, typing, or driving are learned through repetition. With practice, control shifts from conscious processing to automatic execution. The experience is stored as a pattern of coordinated neural activity rather than as explicit knowledge. This is why people can perform complex skills without being able to explain how they do them.

Semantic memory, which involves general knowledge and concepts, is formed through repeated exposure and abstraction. Individual experiences are distilled into generalized representations. Over time, the brain extracts patterns and meanings while discarding contextual details. This process allows efficient thinking but also leads to overgeneralization. The mind remembers "what usually happens" rather than "what happened this time."

Autobiographical memory combines episodic and semantic elements to form personal narratives. These narratives shape identity by organizing experiences into coherent stories. The brain selectively stores and emphasizes experiences that fit existing self-concepts. Over time, memory becomes aligned with identity, reinforcing consistent ways of thinking and interpreting events. Experiences that contradict the narrative may be forgotten or reinterpreted.

Repetition plays a decisive role in storage strength. Experiences that are revisited—through reflection, conversation, or rumination—are stored more robustly. Each reactivation strengthens the associated neural pathways. This applies equally to constructive reflection and maladaptive rumination. The brain does not distinguish between healthy and unhealthy repetition; it strengthens whatever is rehearsed.

Context also influences how experiences are stored and retrieved. Memories are encoded alongside environmental, emotional, and physiological cues. These cues later serve as triggers for recall. This is why certain places, smells, or emotional states can evoke vivid memories unexpectedly. The brain uses context to organize experiences and predict relevance.

Importantly, forgetting is not a failure of memory but a feature of it. The brain actively prunes unused connections to maintain efficiency. Experiences that are not revisited gradually lose accessibility. This process allows the brain to prioritize relevant information but also contributes to memory bias. What is remembered most is not what is most accurate, but what is most reinforced.

The storage of experience is deeply shaped by interpretation. The meaning assigned to an event influences how it is encoded and recalled. Two people can experience the same event and store it differently based on their beliefs, expectations, and emotional states. Memory reflects subjective interpretation more than objective reality.

Traumatic experiences illustrate both the power and the limits of memory storage. Trauma can lead to fragmented or intrusive memories. In some cases, sensory and emotional elements are stored without coherent narrative integration. This results in repeated reactivation without resolution. The brain remains locked in a loop because the experience has not been fully integrated into memory networks.

Understanding how experiences are stored in the brain reveals why thinking patterns are so persistent. Thoughts are not abstract ideas floating freely; they are expressions of stored experience. Each thought reactivates memory networks shaped by past exposure, emotion, and reinforcement. The mind thinks the way it remembers.

This understanding also clarifies why change requires more than insight. New experiences must be encoded, consolidated, and repeated to compete with existing memory structures. Intellectual understanding alone does not overwrite stored experience. The brain changes through repeated activation, not explanation.

Ultimately, experiences are stored in the brain as patterns of connection, not as recordings of reality. Memory is adaptive, selective, and reconstructive. It shapes perception, guides behavior, and anchors identity. By understanding how experiences are stored, individuals gain insight into why certain thoughts recur and why change takes time. The architecture of memory is the architecture of thought.

Emotional Weight and Memory Strength

Not all experiences are remembered equally. Some fade quickly, leaving little trace, while others persist for years, returning vividly and effortlessly to the mind. The difference is rarely the objective importance of the event itself. Instead, it is the emotional weight attached to the experience that determines how strongly it is stored and how often it is recalled. Emotion acts as a multiplier in memory formation, amplifying certain experiences and embedding them deeply into the architecture of thought.

The brain treats emotion as a signal of relevance. From an evolutionary perspective, emotionally charged experiences—those involving danger, reward, attachment, or loss—carried important survival information. As a result, the brain evolved to prioritize their storage. When an experience triggers strong emotion, multiple neural systems activate simultaneously, increasing the likelihood that the experience will be encoded, consolidated, and retrieved later. Memory strength, therefore, is not a measure of accuracy but of emotional significance.

At the center of this process is the interaction between emotional and memory-related brain regions. Emotional arousal activates systems responsible for alertness and stress regulation, which in turn influence how memories are formed. Neurochemical changes during emotional events enhance neural plasticity, making connections more likely to strengthen. This biological response ensures that emotionally significant experiences leave durable traces.

However, emotional weight does not enhance memory uniformly. It strengthens certain aspects of an experience while weakening others. The emotional core—the feeling associated with the event—is often remembered more reliably than specific details such as timing, sequence, or context. This selective strengthening explains why people vividly recall how an event made them feel while disagreeing about what actually happened. Memory prioritizes meaning over precision.

Fear provides a clear illustration. Fear-based memories are often exceptionally strong because they are tied to survival mechanisms. When fear is experienced, the brain rapidly encodes cues associated with potential threat. These cues become triggers for future responses, allowing rapid reaction without deliberation. While this system is adaptive, it can also lead to overgeneralization. Neutral situations that resemble the original threat may activate the same fear memory, even when no danger exists.

Pleasure and reward also carry emotional weight, reinforcing memory through positive association. Experiences that produce pleasure, relief, or approval are likely to be revisited mentally. Each recall strengthens the associated pathways, increasing the probability of repetition. Over time, the mind becomes oriented toward experiences that previously produced positive emotional outcomes, shaping motivation and preference.

Negative emotions such as shame, guilt, and rejection are particularly potent in memory formation. These emotions are deeply tied to social survival. Experiences involving social pain are often replayed repeatedly as the mind attempts to prevent future harm. Each replay reinforces the memory, embedding it more deeply. The brain treats social threat as a critical signal, strengthening the associated memory regardless of its long-term usefulness.

Importantly, emotional intensity does not guarantee healthy memory integration. Highly charged experiences can be stored in fragmented or distorted forms. In such cases, sensory and emotional elements are preserved while contextual understanding remains incomplete. This fragmentation contributes to intrusive memories and repeated thought loops. The mind continues to revisit the experience not to understand it, but because its emotional charge demands attention.

Emotion also influences how often memories are recalled. Emotionally weighted memories are more accessible because they are linked to internal states that recur. A similar emotion in the present can trigger recall of past experiences associated with that emotion. This creates mood-congruent memory, where the mind retrieves memories that match its current emotional state. Over time, this reinforces emotional patterns, shaping perception and interpretation.

Repetition further strengthens emotionally charged memories. Each recall reactivates the associated neural pathways, reinforcing them through reconsolidation. The memory is not simply replayed; it is re-stored, often with added emotional or interpretive layers. This process explains why memories can become more emotionally charged over time rather than fading. Repetition amplifies emotional weight.

Language plays a significant role in this amplification. Emotional experiences are often rehearsed through storytelling, internal dialogue, or rumination. Each verbalization reinforces the memory and solidifies its narrative structure. Over time, the story becomes more stable, and the emotional meaning becomes more entrenched. The memory feels increasingly real, even as details drift from the original event.

Social reinforcement also contributes to memory strength. When emotional experiences are shared and validated by others, their significance is reinforced. Agreement confirms interpretation, while attention rewards recall. As a result, socially reinforced emotional memories become especially persistent. The mind learns which memories are worth keeping alive.

However, emotional weight can distort judgment. Strongly remembered experiences exert disproportionate influence on decision-making. The mind overestimates the likelihood or importance of events that are emotionally vivid. This bias affects risk assessment, belief formation, and expectation. What is remembered most strongly feels most representative, even when it is not.

This distortion explains why emotionally charged beliefs are resistant to change. Challenging them threatens not just an idea, but a deeply reinforced memory network. The mind reacts defensively because the memory feels foundational. Logical arguments often fail because they do not address the emotional reinforcement underlying the belief.

Understanding emotional weight also clarifies why insight alone rarely produces change. Even when individuals recognize that a belief is inaccurate, the emotional memory supporting it may remain intact. The brain continues to activate the familiar pattern because it has been reinforced repeatedly. Change requires new emotional experiences that compete with existing ones.

Positive emotional reinforcement can be used deliberately to reshape memory. When reflection, learning, or new interpretations are paired with satisfaction or relief, they become more likely to be remembered and repeated. Over time, healthier patterns can gain emotional weight, gradually weakening older ones through disuse.

Emotional regulation plays a crucial role in this process. When emotional intensity is reduced, memory retrieval becomes more flexible. The mind is better able to re-evaluate past experiences and integrate them into broader understanding. Calm states support reconsolidation that updates memory rather than reinforcing it rigidly.

Importantly, emotional weight does not imply permanence. While emotionally charged memories are strong, they are not fixed. Neuroplasticity allows memory networks to change with repeated experience. However, this change requires time, repetition, and emotional engagement. The brain does not release what it has learned to protect without learning something else in its place.

Ultimately, emotional weight determines memory strength because emotion signals importance. The brain remembers what it believes matters. This mechanism has allowed humans to survive, learn, and adapt, but it also explains why certain thoughts repeat endlessly. The mind is guided less by what is true than by what has been emotionally reinforced.

Recognizing the role of emotion in memory formation restores perspective. It reveals that persistent thoughts are not failures of willpower or intelligence, but the result of learned emotional priorities. By understanding how emotional weight shapes memory strength, individuals gain the ability to work with the mind rather than against it. Memory can be retrained, but only by respecting the emotional forces that built it.

Why the Mind Replays the Past

The human mind has a persistent tendency to return to past experiences. Moments of embarrassment resurface uninvited, painful events replay repeatedly, and even joyful memories reappear with striking clarity. This replaying of the past is often misunderstood as weakness, nostalgia, or lack of control. In reality, it is a fundamental function of how the mind learns, predicts, and protects itself. The mind replays the past not to trap us in it, but because memory is the primary tool through which the brain prepares for the future.

At its core, the brain is a predictive organ. Its central task is not to remember for remembrance's sake, but to anticipate what might happen next. Past experiences provide the data for these predictions. When the mind replays an event, it is often attempting to extract patterns, refine expectations, or prevent future harm. The replay is not random; it is driven by perceived relevance. The brain revisits what it believes still matters.

Emotional significance is the strongest trigger for replay. Experiences associated with fear, shame, loss, pleasure, or reward signal importance. These emotions tell the brain, "Pay attention—this could happen again." As a result, emotionally charged memories are recalled more frequently. Each replay strengthens the associated neural pathways, making future recall easier and more automatic. The memory persists not because it is unresolved, but because it has been tagged as significant.

Uncertainty intensifies replay. When an experience lacks closure or clear meaning, the mind continues to revisit it. The brain dislikes ambiguity. Replay becomes an attempt to resolve unanswered questions: Why did this happen? What did I miss? How could it have gone differently? The mind reprocesses the event repeatedly, searching for insight or control. Until a satisfying interpretation is found, the memory remains active.

Replay also serves learning. The brain refines behavior by simulating past outcomes. By replaying experiences, the mind strengthens associations between actions and consequences. This mechanism is essential for skill acquisition and decision-making. Athletes mentally rehearse past performances to improve future ones.

Similarly, the mind replays everyday experiences to adjust expectations and responses. What feels like rumination is often the brain's effort to optimize behavior.

However, replay does not always produce improvement. When the same interpretation is rehearsed repeatedly without variation, the mind becomes trapped in a loop. The brain strengthens the emotional response rather than extracting new insight. In these cases, replay reinforces distress instead of learning. The mechanism remains adaptive in intent, but maladaptive in outcome.

Identity plays a significant role in why the mind replays certain memories. Experiences that threaten or confirm one's self-concept are especially likely to be revisited. The mind uses memory to maintain a coherent narrative of who we are. Events that challenge this narrative demand attention. Replay becomes a way to integrate the experience into identity—or to defend against its implications. The past is replayed not as history, but as evidence.

Social experiences are particularly prone to replay. Human beings are deeply sensitive to social evaluation. Memories involving rejection, humiliation, or conflict are often replayed because they carry implications for belonging and status. The brain treats social pain as a serious threat, activating the same systems involved in physical danger. Replay becomes a way to prevent future social harm by analyzing past interactions.

Language intensifies replay. Once an experience is translated into words, it becomes easier to rehearse. Internal dialogue turns memory into narrative, and narrative invites repetition. Each time the story is told—internally or externally—it becomes more structured and more accessible. Over time, the mind remembers the story more than the original event. Replay becomes habitual, not because the event is ongoing, but because the narrative is.

Memory replay is also influenced by current emotional states. The mind tends to retrieve memories that match how it feels. When sad, past sadness comes to mind. When anxious, past threats resurface. This mood-congruent recall creates feedback loops in which present emotion triggers past memory, and past memory reinforces present emotion. The replay feels involuntary, but it follows predictable patterns.

Importantly, the mind replays the past to maintain predictability. Familiar pain is less threatening than unknown pain. By revisiting known outcomes, the brain preserves a sense of control. Letting go of a memory means facing uncertainty. Replay, even when unpleasant, provides structure. The mind prefers a painful certainty over an undefined future.

This explains why insight alone does not stop replay. Understanding that a memory is unhelpful does not immediately weaken the neural pathways that support it. Replay is driven by repetition, not logic. Each time the memory is revisited, the pathway is reinforced. The brain learns through activation, not intention. To reduce replay, new patterns must compete with old ones through repeated engagement.

Replay also persists when an experience has not been emotionally integrated. Integration occurs when an event is placed into a broader understanding that reduces its emotional charge. Without integration, the memory remains isolated and reactive. The brain continues to revisit it because it has not been fully processed. Replay is the mind's attempt to finish unfinished work.

Sleep provides further insight into this process. During sleep, the brain replays recent experiences to consolidate memory. This replay is essential for learning. However, emotionally intense memories may be replayed more frequently, both during sleep and waking life. When emotional regulation is compromised, these replays spill into conscious awareness as intrusive thoughts.

Modern environments exacerbate mental replay. Constant stimulation, distraction, and information overload reduce opportunities for reflective processing. Experiences are accumulated faster than they are integrated. As a result, unresolved memories accumulate, demanding replay. The mind has not changed, but the pace of experience has.

Understanding why the mind replays the past reframes the experience. Replay is not evidence of weakness or obsession; it is evidence of learning mechanisms at work. The problem is not that the mind replays, but how it replays. When replay is rigid and emotionally charged, it reinforces distress. When replay is reflective and contextualized, it supports growth.

Reducing unhelpful replay does not mean suppressing memory. Suppression often strengthens the very patterns it seeks to eliminate. Instead, change occurs through altered engagement. Introducing new interpretations, emotional regulation, and broader context during recall can gradually weaken the loop. Each updated replay reshapes the memory through reconsolidation.

Ultimately, the mind replays the past because memory is the foundation of prediction. The brain returns to what it has learned in order to navigate what lies ahead. Replay is not the enemy of progress; it is a mechanism awaiting guidance. When the mind is taught to replay with awareness rather than reflex, memory becomes a source of wisdom rather than repetition.

Recall, Reconstruction, and Mental Shortcuts

Memory is often imagined as a retrieval system that pulls intact records of the past into the present. In reality, recall is not a process of replay but one of reconstruction. Each time the mind remembers, it actively rebuilds an experience using fragments stored across neural networks, guided by current beliefs, emotions, and expectations. This reconstructive nature of memory explains why recollection is efficient, flexible, and adaptive—and also why it is vulnerable to distortion. Mental shortcuts play a central role in this process, allowing the brain to remember quickly rather than accurately.

Recall begins when a cue—internal or external—activates related neural pathways. A smell, a word, an emotional state, or a situational similarity can trigger memory retrieval. The brain does not search for a complete record. Instead, it activates associated elements: sensory impressions, emotional tones, contextual details, and narrative meaning. These elements are then assembled into a coherent experience that feels like a faithful memory, even though it is a reconstruction shaped by the present moment.

This process is efficient because the brain prioritizes meaning over detail. Storing and retrieving exact replicas of experience would be metabolically expensive and cognitively impractical. Reconstruction allows the mind to extract what seems relevant and discard what appears unnecessary. The cost of this efficiency is precision. Memory fills in gaps using assumptions, patterns, and expectations derived from past learning.

Mental shortcuts—also known as heuristics—are central to reconstruction. These shortcuts are learned rules of thumb that simplify complex cognitive tasks. During recall, they help the brain infer missing information quickly. If certain details are vague or absent, the mind substitutes what usually happens, what fits the narrative, or what aligns with existing beliefs. The resulting memory feels complete, even when it contains inferred elements rather than stored ones.

Schemas play a critical role in this process. Schemas are organized frameworks of knowledge that represent typical patterns—how events usually unfold, how people usually behave, or what outcomes are expected. During reconstruction, schemas guide recall by providing structure. If an experience fits a known schema, recall becomes easier and faster. However, schema-driven recall also introduces bias. Details that align with the schema are emphasized, while details that contradict it are minimized or omitted.

Emotion strongly influences reconstruction. Emotional states at the time of recall shape which elements are emphasized. A person recalling an event while anxious may reconstruct it as more threatening than it originally was. When recalling the same event while calm, the memory may appear less intense or more nuanced. The experience itself has not changed, but the reconstruction has. Memory reflects current state as much as past reality.

Each act of recall modifies the memory through a process known as reconsolidation. When a memory is retrieved, it becomes temporarily malleable before being stored again. During this window, new information, interpretations, or emotions can be incorporated. This means that remembering is also a form of learning. Over time, repeated recall can significantly alter a memory, reinforcing certain aspects while reshaping others. The memory becomes a record not only of the original experience, but of every time it has been remembered.

Mental shortcuts make this process manageable. Without them, recall would be slow and cognitively demanding. Shortcuts allow the brain to prioritize speed and coherence. For example, the mind often remembers the gist of an event rather than its specifics. This gist-based recall supports understanding and communication, but it sacrifices detail. The remembered story becomes smoother and more consistent with existing beliefs.

This mechanism explains why confidence in memory does not correlate strongly with accuracy. A memory that is reconstructed fluently feels certain because the shortcuts work smoothly. Difficulty recalling details creates doubt, while ease creates confidence. The mind interprets fluency as reliability. In reality, fluency often reflects familiarity with the narrative rather than fidelity to the original event.

Recall is also influenced by repetition. Memories that are recalled frequently become more accessible, not necessarily more accurate. Each reconstruction strengthens the pathways involved, making recall faster the next time. At the same time, inferred elements introduced during reconstruction become part of the memory. Over time, the boundary between what was experienced and what was inferred dissolves. The memory feels stable, even as it drifts from the original event.

Language plays a powerful role in shaping reconstruction. Memories are often encoded and retrieved through verbal narratives. Repeated descriptions solidify certain interpretations. Over time, the story becomes more polished and consistent, while ambiguities are resolved in favor of coherence. The mind remembers the story it has told, not the raw experience. Language acts as both a shortcut and a constraint.

Social factors further reinforce these processes. When memories are shared, feedback from others influences reconstruction. Agreement validates the narrative; disagreement prompts adjustment. Social reinforcement strengthens certain versions of memory while weakening others. Collective remembering shapes individual recall. The memory becomes aligned with shared narratives rather than private experience.

Mental shortcuts are especially influential under cognitive load. When attention, time, or emotional regulation is limited, the brain relies more heavily on schemas and heuristics. Recall becomes faster but less flexible. This is why stressful or emotionally charged contexts often produce rigid, simplified memories. The mind prioritizes resolution over nuance.

These mechanisms have important implications for thinking. Because recall shapes perception, reconstructed memories influence how new experiences are interpreted. The mind does not approach situations neutrally; it approaches them with expectations derived from memory. Shortcuts allow rapid interpretation, but they also perpetuate repetition. The same patterns are activated again and again, reinforcing familiar ways of thinking.

Importantly, reconstruction is not a flaw; it is a feature. It allows the mind to adapt, generalize, and learn from experience. The problem arises when reconstructed memories are mistaken for objective records. When this happens, individuals may defend memories as facts rather than interpretations. Critical reflection becomes difficult because the memory feels authoritative.

Understanding recall as reconstruction restores flexibility. It reveals that memories are not fixed truths but evolving representations. This understanding makes it possible to revisit memories with curiosity rather than certainty. By slowing down recall, examining assumptions, and questioning shortcuts, individuals can weaken rigid patterns and allow more accurate understanding to emerge.

Change requires engaging with memory differently. Instead of rehearsing familiar narratives, new interpretations must be introduced during recall. This does not erase the past, but it updates its meaning. Over time, repeated reflective recall can reshape memory networks, reducing the dominance of unhelpful shortcuts.

Ultimately, recall, reconstruction, and mental shortcuts explain why thinking is so often repetitive. The mind relies on what it remembers, and it remembers through efficient reconstruction. Thoughts repeat not because the mind is lazy or irrational, but because it is optimized for speed and coherence. By understanding this process, individuals gain the ability to interrupt repetition and introduce reflection. Memory remains the architect of thought, but its designs are not beyond revision.

Chapter 4

Conditioning the Way We Think

Thinking does not develop in isolation. Long before individuals form deliberate opinions or conscious beliefs, their minds are shaped by patterns of reinforcement, reward, and response. This process—known as conditioning—quietly trains how people interpret experiences, react emotionally, and draw conclusions. By the time thinking feels personal and self-directed, much of its structure has already been conditioned by past exposure and repeated outcomes.

Conditioning refers to the way the mind learns associations between events, behaviors, and consequences. When certain thoughts, interpretations, or reactions consistently produce relief, approval, or success, they are reinforced. When others lead to discomfort, rejection, or failure, they are weakened or suppressed. Over time, the mind learns which patterns are "safe" and which are risky. These learned patterns become automatic, guiding thought without conscious awareness.

This conditioning begins early. In childhood, caregivers, educators, and environments reward some ways of thinking while discouraging others. Curiosity may be praised or dismissed.

Questioning may be encouraged or punished. Emotional expression may be accepted or restricted. Each response teaches the mind what kinds of thoughts are permissible and effective. The child does not reason about these outcomes; the brain simply adapts.

As conditioning continues, thinking becomes linked to emotion. Certain ideas feel comfortable, while others provoke anxiety or resistance. These emotional signals are not evidence of correctness; they are indicators of learned association. The mind learns not only what to think, but how to feel about thinking in certain ways. Over time, emotion becomes a gatekeeper, guiding which thoughts are pursued and which are avoided.

Conditioning also shapes attention. The mind becomes trained to notice what has mattered before. If certain cues have reliably predicted reward or threat, attention is drawn to them automatically. This selective focus influences interpretation. The mind sees what it has learned to see, reinforcing existing patterns. Conditioning narrows perception long before reasoning begins.

Importantly, conditioning does not require conscious belief. A person may intellectually reject an idea while still reacting to it emotionally because the underlying association remains intact. This explains why insight alone often fails to change behavior. Conditioning operates at a level below rational thought. The brain responds to learned cues even when the conscious mind disagrees.

Social environments are powerful conditioning agents. Approval, belonging, and validation function as strong reinforcers. When certain views align with group norms, they are rewarded through acceptance. When they deviate, discomfort follows. Over time, social conditioning shapes belief systems that feel self-chosen but are deeply influenced by reinforcement history. Thinking becomes synchronized with belonging.

Language plays a critical role in this process. Words carry emotional and social weight. Repeated phrases, labels, and narratives condition interpretation. Over time, language cues trigger automatic responses. A single word can activate an entire belief structure. Conditioning turns language into a shortcut for complex evaluation.

Modern life intensifies conditioning. Constant feedback—likes, comments, metrics, and reactions—trains attention and interpretation continuously. Thoughts that gain engagement are reinforced; those that do not fade. The mind adapts quickly, optimizing for response rather than reflection. Conditioning accelerates, often without awareness.

Understanding conditioning reframes responsibility. It reveals that thinking patterns are not moral failings or intellectual deficiencies, but learned responses. This perspective reduces self-blame and increases agency. If thinking has been conditioned, it can be reconditioned. The mind is not fixed; it is trainable.

This chapter explores how conditioning shapes thought patterns, emotional responses, and belief formation. By examining reward, punishment, social influence, and repetition, we begin to see how thinking becomes predictable. Recognizing conditioning is the first step toward interrupting it. Only by understanding how the mind has been trained can we begin to train it intentionally.

Childhood Programming and Early Beliefs

The foundations of adult thinking are laid long before adulthood begins. Childhood is not merely a developmental stage; it is the primary programming period of the human mind. During these early years, beliefs about the self, others, and the world are formed not through critical evaluation, but through exposure, repetition, and emotional experience. By the time conscious reasoning matures, many core assumptions are already in place, operating silently beneath awareness. These early beliefs become the default settings of thought, shaping perception and behavior throughout life.

Children do not think analytically in the way adults do. Their minds are highly receptive, not skeptical. They absorb patterns without questioning their validity because survival depends on learning quickly from the environment. Caregivers, authority figures, and surroundings become sources of implicit truth. What is repeated, modeled, or emotionally reinforced is accepted as reality. This is not a flaw; it is an adaptive necessity. However, it also means that early beliefs are rarely chosen—they are inherited.

Childhood programming occurs through observation as much as instruction. Children learn how the world works by watching how adults react to success, failure, conflict, and uncertainty. Emotional responses are especially influential. A child who repeatedly observes anxiety around money may internalize beliefs about scarcity and insecurity, even if those beliefs are never spoken aloud. Similarly, a child exposed to calm problem-solving may learn that challenges are manageable. The mind learns not from explanations, but from patterns.

Language plays a central role in early programming. Repeated phrases such as "be careful," "don't ask questions," "you're so smart," or "you always mess things up" shape internal narratives. These phrases are not evaluated for accuracy; they are encoded as identity-relevant information. Over time, external language becomes internal dialogue. The child does not remember when the belief was formed; it simply feels true.

Reward and punishment further reinforce early beliefs. When certain behaviors or expressions are consistently rewarded with attention, approval, or affection, they are repeated. When others are punished or ignored, they are suppressed. The child learns which aspects of themselves are acceptable and which are not. This conditioning shapes not only behavior, but thought. Certain ideas feel safe to entertain; others feel dangerous or forbidden.

Importantly, early beliefs are often global and simplistic. Children lack the cognitive capacity to interpret nuance. As a result, they form broad conclusions from limited experiences. A few instances of rejection may lead to the belief "I am not wanted." A few moments of praise may lead to "I must always perform to be valued." These beliefs are not consciously chosen; they are emotional generalizations formed in the absence of context.

Emotion acts as a powerful cement in this process. Experiences associated with strong emotion are encoded more deeply and recalled more often. Fear, shame, joy, and approval amplify learning. A single emotionally intense event can shape belief more strongly than many neutral ones. The brain prioritizes emotional relevance over statistical accuracy. As a result, early emotionally charged experiences exert disproportionate influence on later thinking.

Attachment relationships are especially influential. Early interactions with caregivers teach the child what to expect from others. Consistent care fosters beliefs about safety and trust. Inconsistent or unpredictable care fosters vigilance and anxiety. These beliefs operate implicitly, shaping how relationships are perceived and navigated later in life. Adult relational patterns often mirror early attachment programming, even when circumstances have changed.

Cultural and social contexts also contribute to childhood programming. Norms regarding gender, authority, success, and morality are absorbed through repetition. The child learns what is valued and what is discouraged. These lessons are rarely explicit. They are embedded in stories, traditions, reactions, and expectations. Over time, cultural beliefs feel natural rather than learned.

Educational environments reinforce this programming. Schools often reward compliance, speed, and correctness rather than curiosity and reflection. Children learn whether questioning is welcome or risky. These experiences shape beliefs about thinking itself. Some children learn that thinking is exploration; others learn that it is performance. These early lessons influence intellectual confidence and engagement throughout life.

One of the most enduring effects of childhood programming is the formation of self-beliefs. Beliefs about intelligence, worth, capability, and belonging become reference points for interpretation. Once formed, these beliefs guide attention and memory. Experiences that confirm them are noticed and remembered; those that contradict them are minimized or reinterpreted. The belief becomes self-reinforcing, not because it is accurate, but because it organizes perception.

Importantly, childhood beliefs are often implicit. Adults may not consciously endorse them, yet still act as if they are true. A person may intellectually believe they are competent while emotionally reacting as if they are inadequate. This discrepancy reflects the difference between later reasoning and early programming. The belief was learned before reasoning was available to evaluate it.

This explains why insight alone often fails to produce change. Understanding that a belief is outdated or inaccurate does not automatically deactivate the emotional and neural patterns that support it. Early programming operates at a deeper level, shaped by repetition and reinforcement rather than logic. Change requires engaging the same mechanisms through which the belief was formed.

Memory plays a critical role in maintaining early beliefs. Childhood experiences are recalled selectively, reinforcing existing narratives. Over time, memory becomes aligned with belief rather than reality. The past is remembered in ways that support current identity. This process is largely unconscious, yet highly influential.

However, early programming is not destiny. The brain remains plastic throughout life. While early beliefs are deeply ingrained, they are not immutable. New experiences, repeated consistently and paired with emotional engagement, can reshape thinking patterns. This process is gradual and requires patience, but it is possible.

Recognizing childhood programming reframes self-understanding. It shifts the narrative from personal failure to learned adaptation. Beliefs that once served survival may no longer serve growth. Understanding their origin reduces shame and opens the door to change. The goal is not to blame the past, but to understand its influence.

Ultimately, childhood programming and early beliefs form the blueprint of adult thinking. They shape what feels possible, what feels threatening, and what feels true. By bringing these patterns into awareness, individuals gain the opportunity to update them. The mind may have been programmed early, but it is not locked forever. Conscious repetition can rewrite unconscious beliefs, transforming inherited patterns into chosen ones.

Reward, Punishment, and Mental Training

The human mind is shaped less by instruction than by consequence. What is rewarded tends to repeat. What is punished tends to disappear—or, in some cases, retreat underground. This simple principle governs behavior, emotion, and thought alike. From early childhood through adulthood, reward and punishment function as the primary tools through which the mind is trained. Over time, these mechanisms sculpt not only what people do, but how they think.

Mental training through reward and punishment operates largely outside conscious awareness. The brain continuously evaluates outcomes, registering which thoughts, interpretations, and reactions lead to comfort, approval, relief, or success, and which lead to discomfort, rejection, or failure. Patterns associated with positive outcomes are reinforced; those associated with negative outcomes are weakened or avoided. This process does not require reflection or intention. It is automatic learning.

Reward strengthens mental patterns by signaling effectiveness. When a particular way of thinking produces a desirable result—such as praise, validation, emotional relief, or a sense of control—the brain marks that pattern as useful. Neural pathways associated with that thought are reinforced, making them more likely to activate again. Over time, the thought becomes habitual, arising quickly and effortlessly. The individual experiences it as natural or intuitive, unaware that it has been trained through repetition and reinforcement.

Punishment operates differently but just as powerfully. When a thought or expression leads to embarrassment, rejection, fear, or loss, the brain learns to inhibit it. This does not always eliminate the thought itself. Instead, it may suppress its expression or redirect it into safer forms. Punishment trains avoidance rather than understanding. The mind learns what not to think openly, not necessarily what is inaccurate.

Importantly, reward and punishment do not discriminate between healthy and unhealthy patterns. A belief that reduces anxiety may be rewarded through emotional relief, even if it distorts reality. Avoidance may be rewarded by reduced discomfort, even if it prevents growth. The brain optimizes for immediate outcomes, not long-term accuracy or well-being. What feels better now is reinforced, regardless of future cost.

Early mental training often relies heavily on punishment. Children learn quickly which thoughts, questions, or emotions provoke negative reactions from authority figures. Over time, these experiences condition internal boundaries. Certain ideas feel unsafe to explore, while others feel acceptable. This conditioning shapes intellectual curiosity, emotional expression, and self-trust. The child does not analyze these patterns; the brain simply adapts.

Reward-based training can be equally limiting. When approval is tied to performance, compliance, or agreement, the mind learns to associate worth with specific outcomes. Thinking becomes goal-oriented rather than exploratory. The individual learns to think in ways that gain reward rather than in ways that seek understanding. Over time, this produces mental rigidity masked as competence.

Educational systems often reinforce these dynamics. Correct answers are rewarded; incorrect ones are punished or ignored. Speed is praised; hesitation is discouraged. As a result, students learn to value certainty over inquiry. Thinking becomes a performance rather than a process. The reward structure trains recall and pattern matching more than reasoning. Punishment discourages experimentation and doubt.

Social environments extend this training into adulthood. Agreement brings acceptance; disagreement risks exclusion. Certain opinions are rewarded with validation, while others are punished with ridicule or isolation. The mind adapts by aligning thought with social norms. Over time, socially rewarded beliefs feel personally chosen. The individual experiences conformity as conviction.

Internal rewards and punishments are just as influential. Thoughts that reduce internal tension are rewarded with relief. Thoughts that provoke guilt or anxiety are punished internally. This creates self-reinforcing loops. Rationalizations reduce discomfort and are repeated. Self-criticism may be punished or, paradoxically, rewarded if it aligns with learned identity. The mind trains itself continuously through internal feedback.

Emotion plays a central role in this process. Emotional responses act as immediate feedback signals. Pleasure, pride, relief, and safety reinforce thought patterns. Fear, shame, and anxiety suppress or redirect them. Because emotion operates faster than conscious reasoning, emotional reinforcement often overrides rational evaluation. The mind learns emotionally before it understands intellectually.

Over time, reward and punishment shape attention. The mind becomes trained to notice what leads to reward and avoid what leads to punishment. This selective attention reinforces existing patterns further. Certain cues become salient; others fade from awareness. Thinking narrows, not by conscious choice, but by conditioned focus.

Mental training through punishment can produce rigidity and avoidance. Thoughts associated with past punishment may trigger anxiety before they are fully formed. The individual avoids questioning, creativity, or emotional honesty not because these are harmful, but because they were once penalized. The punishment persists long after the original context has changed.

Reward-based training can also backfire. When thinking is rewarded for being quick, confident, or aligned with authority, deeper reasoning is discouraged. The mind becomes skilled at producing acceptable answers rather than accurate ones. Over time, this creates overconfidence and resistance to feedback. Reward strengthens certainty, not insight.

Crucially, reward and punishment shape identity. Repeated reinforcement teaches the mind not only what to think, but who it is allowed to be. Thoughts become associated with self-worth. Challenging a belief feels like risking identity. The mind defends trained patterns because they have been tied to reward and safety.

Understanding this process reframes change. Unhelpful thinking patterns persist not because of weakness or stubbornness, but because they have been reinforced repeatedly. Insight alone rarely dismantles them because insight does not alter reinforcement. The brain changes through consequences, not conclusions.

Effective mental retraining requires adjusting reward structures. Reflective thinking must become rewarding. Curiosity must be associated with satisfaction rather than anxiety. Errors must be treated as information rather than punishment. Without this shift, new thinking patterns cannot compete with old ones.

This retraining takes time. Established patterns have been reinforced over years. New patterns require repeated activation paired with positive reinforcement. Each instance of choosing reflection over reaction, curiosity over certainty, must be experienced as worthwhile. Over time, new habits form.

Punishment must also be softened. Reducing internal and external penalties for uncertainty creates space for growth. When the mind no longer associates questioning with threat, it becomes more flexible. Safety enables exploration. Without safety, thinking remains defensive.

Ultimately, reward and punishment are the tools through which the mind is trained. They shape attention, belief, and identity more powerfully than instruction ever could. By becoming aware of these forces, individuals gain the ability to redesign their mental training. Thinking becomes intentional rather than conditioned. The mind is not fixed by what it has learned—it is shaped by what it continues to reward.

Social Conditioning and Cultural Scripts

Human thinking does not emerge in a vacuum. It is shaped continuously by the social environments in which individuals live and by the cultural scripts that define what is normal, acceptable, admirable, or dangerous. Social conditioning and cultural scripts operate as invisible frameworks that guide interpretation, behavior, and belief long before conscious reasoning has a chance to intervene. Most people experience their thoughts as personal and self-generated, yet a significant portion of what feels like independent thinking is, in reality, socially trained cognition.

Social conditioning refers to the process through which individuals learn how to think, feel, and respond based on social feedback. Approval, disapproval, inclusion, exclusion, praise, ridicule, and silence all function as conditioning tools. From early childhood, the mind learns which thoughts gain acceptance and which create friction. Over time, this learning becomes internalized. External social rules transform into internal mental boundaries.

Cultural scripts are the narratives, assumptions, and expectations embedded within a society. They define roles, values, and interpretations. Scripts answer implicit questions such as: What does success look like? Who deserves respect? What is considered normal behavior? What emotions are acceptable to express? These scripts are not usually taught explicitly. They are absorbed through repetition—stories, traditions, media, language, rituals, and everyday interactions. Once internalized, they guide thinking automatically.

The power of social conditioning lies in its subtlety. Rarely does a society announce its rules openly. Instead, it rewards conformity and penalizes deviation. When an individual expresses a belief that aligns with group norms, they are met with agreement or approval. When they diverge, they may encounter discomfort, dismissal, or isolation. The brain learns quickly from these outcomes. Beliefs associated with belonging are reinforced. Those associated with social risk are suppressed or reshaped.

Belonging is one of the strongest human motivators. The brain treats social acceptance as a form of safety. As a result, thinking becomes aligned with group identity. Individuals often adopt shared beliefs not because they have evaluated them, but because they signal membership. Over time, these beliefs feel personal. The line between "what I think" and "what we think" disappears. Social conditioning becomes self-conditioning.

Cultural scripts provide cognitive shortcuts. They simplify complex realities into familiar stories. For example, scripts about gender, success, authority, morality, or intelligence offer ready-made interpretations. These interpretations reduce uncertainty and cognitive effort. Rather than analyzing each situation independently, the mind applies a known script. The result is efficiency, but also rigidity. Scripts discourage questioning by presenting assumptions as obvious truths.

Language is a primary carrier of cultural scripts. Repeated phrases, metaphors, and labels shape perception. Certain words trigger entire frameworks of meaning. Over time, language trains thought. The mind reacts not to reality itself, but to the linguistic categories used to describe it. Once a situation is labeled, interpretation follows automatically. Cultural scripts operate through language long before conscious reasoning begins.

Media plays a powerful role in reinforcing these scripts. Repeated representations of certain roles, values, and narratives normalize specific ways of thinking. Exposure alone is enough to train perception. What is shown repeatedly becomes familiar. What is familiar feels normal. What feels normal feels true. This process does not require persuasion; it requires repetition.

Social conditioning also shapes emotional responses. Cultural scripts teach individuals not only what to think, but how to feel. Some emotions are encouraged, others discouraged. Pride may be rewarded in some contexts and punished in others. Anger may be acceptable for certain groups and unacceptable for others. Over time, emotional responses become conditioned. Feelings arise automatically in response to scripted situations.

Importantly, social conditioning does not eliminate individuality. Instead, it channels it. Individuals express uniqueness within culturally acceptable boundaries. Creativity is permitted where it does not threaten core scripts. Dissent is tolerated when it remains symbolic rather than disruptive. The mind learns where freedom exists and where it does not. These boundaries feel internal, not imposed.

Cultural scripts are reinforced through repetition across generations. Children absorb them through observation long before they understand them. What adults model becomes reality. What is praised becomes desirable. What is ignored becomes irrelevant. By adulthood, many scripts feel timeless and self-evident. Their historical and cultural origins fade from awareness.

One of the most powerful effects of social conditioning is the illusion of independent belief. Because scripts are learned gradually and reinforced socially, individuals experience them as personal convictions. Questioning them feels unnatural or even immoral. The discomfort that arises when a script is challenged is often interpreted as evidence that the challenge is wrong. In reality, it is evidence of conditioning.

Social conditioning also explains why certain ideas feel threatening even when they pose no direct harm. Challenges to cultural scripts destabilize shared meaning. They introduce uncertainty not only about facts, but about identity and belonging. The mind reacts defensively because the script has been tied to safety. Logic alone cannot overcome this reaction because the resistance is emotional and social, not intellectual.

Education often reinforces cultural scripts rather than questioning them. Curricula emphasize accepted knowledge and standardized interpretations. Critical examination of foundational assumptions is rare. As a result, learners become proficient in applying scripts rather than evaluating them. Pattern recognition is rewarded; critical reasoning is constrained.

Workplaces further entrench these patterns. Organizational cultures reward specific ways of thinking, speaking, and problem-solving. Individuals adapt their cognition to fit expectations. Over time, professional identity shapes thought. Certain questions are never asked because they fall outside the script. Innovation is encouraged only within predefined limits.

Understanding social conditioning does not require rejecting culture or society. Scripts are necessary for coordination and shared meaning. The danger lies in mistaking scripts for universal truth. When cultural assumptions go unexamined, they limit perception and constrain thinking. Awareness restores choice.

Breaking free from rigid scripts does not mean abandoning belonging. It means recognizing influence. When individuals understand how their thinking has been shaped, they gain the ability to pause, question, and evaluate. This does not require constant skepticism, but selective awareness. Some scripts serve growth; others preserve stagnation.

Change begins with noticing patterns of agreement and discomfort. Which ideas feel safe? Which feel forbidden? These emotional signals point to conditioning. By examining them rather than obeying them automatically, the mind creates space for reflection. New ways of thinking can emerge gradually.

Ultimately, social conditioning and cultural scripts shape thinking by defining what feels normal, true, and acceptable. They operate through repetition, reinforcement, and belonging. Recognizing their influence does not weaken the mind; it strengthens it. When individuals understand the scripts they have inherited, they gain the power to choose which ones to keep and which ones to revise. Thinking becomes less reactive and more intentional. The mind remains social, but it is no longer confined by invisible rules it did not choose.

How Authority Shapes Thought Habits

Authority plays a decisive role in shaping how people think, often more powerfully than evidence or personal experience. From childhood onward, human beings are trained to associate authority with correctness, safety, and legitimacy. Over time, this association becomes embedded in mental habits, guiding interpretation, belief formation, and decision-making. Thought habits shaped by authority often operate automatically, long after the original authority figure is no longer present.

Authority influences thinking because the human brain evolved in social hierarchies. Survival historically depended on learning quickly from those with power, knowledge, or status. Questioning authority carried risk; compliance offered protection. As a result, the brain developed a bias toward accepting information from perceived authority figures without requiring independent verification. This bias is not a flaw of intelligence but a feature of social adaptation.

Early authority figures—parents, caregivers, and teachers—play a foundational role in shaping thought habits. Children lack the cognitive capacity to evaluate claims critically, so they rely on authority as a proxy for truth. What authority figures say is accepted as reality, not opinion. Repetition strengthens this association. Over time, authority-linked beliefs feel self-evident rather than learned.

This dynamic extends beyond content into process. Authority does not only shape what is thought, but how thinking occurs. Children learn whether questioning is encouraged or punished. In environments where authority discourages inquiry, thinking becomes cautious and externally guided. In environments where authority welcomes exploration, thinking becomes flexible and self-directed. These patterns persist into adulthood as default thinking styles.

Educational systems institutionalize authority-based thinking. Curricula, grading systems, and standardized assessments reinforce the idea that correct answers originate from approved sources. Students are rewarded for reproducing sanctioned knowledge rather than interrogating assumptions. Over time, many learners internalize the belief that thinking means recalling authoritative information, not evaluating it. This habit can persist even in advanced intellectual settings.

Authority also shapes thinking through emotional conditioning. Approval from authority figures functions as a powerful reward. Disapproval triggers anxiety, shame, or fear. The brain associates certain thoughts with safety and others with threat. Once this association is formed, authority no longer needs to be present. The mind self-regulates, suppressing thoughts that once carried risk and favoring those that once earned approval.

Language reinforces this process. Statements delivered with authority are often framed as definitive rather than tentative. Certainty signals competence. Over time, the mind learns to equate confidence with correctness. Ideas expressed hesitantly are discounted, while those delivered assertively are accepted. This habit distorts evaluation by privileging tone over substance.

Social authority amplifies these effects. Leaders, experts, institutions, and cultural icons shape collective belief through visibility and repetition. When authoritative voices repeat certain narratives, they become normalized. Dissenting views are marginalized not through refutation, but through absence of authority endorsement. The mind interprets silence as invalidation.

Importantly, authority shapes not only beliefs, but the boundaries of thought. Certain questions are never asked because authority has implicitly defined them as inappropriate, irrelevant, or dangerous. These boundaries feel internal rather than imposed. Individuals may believe they are thinking freely while operating entirely within authority-defined limits.

Authority-based thought habits also explain why contradictory evidence is often dismissed. When evidence conflicts with authoritative belief, the mind experiences cognitive tension. Because authority has been associated with safety and correctness, challenging it feels risky. The brain resolves this tension by discrediting the evidence rather than revising the belief. This response is emotional before it is intellectual.

Workplace hierarchies further reinforce authority-shaped thinking. Organizational cultures reward alignment with leadership perspectives. Employees learn quickly which ideas advance careers and which stall them. Over time, thinking adapts to expectations. Innovation becomes constrained to acceptable parameters. Authority defines not only decisions, but imagination.

Authority also influences moral thinking. Ethical frameworks are often inherited from religious, legal, or cultural authorities. These frameworks provide structure and predictability, but they can also inhibit moral reasoning. When morality is outsourced to authority, individuals may follow rules without examining consequences. Thought becomes obedience rather than reflection.

The power of authority is strongest when it is invisible. Explicit authority invites scrutiny; implicit authority bypasses it. When ideas are presented as common sense, tradition, or expert consensus, they avoid evaluation. The mind accepts them as background reality. Authority disappears into normality.

Understanding how authority shapes thought habits does not require rejecting authority entirely. Authority serves essential functions in complex societies. The danger lies in unexamined reliance. When authority replaces reasoning, thinking becomes passive. When authority is treated as input rather than conclusion, thinking remains active.

Developing independence of thought requires recognizing authority's influence. This begins by asking simple questions: Who taught me this? Under what conditions? What was rewarded? What was discouraged? These questions introduce distance between belief and source. Distance enables evaluation.

Healthy thinking involves balancing authority and reasoning. Authority provides knowledge; reasoning determines meaning. Authority offers guidance; reasoning assesses relevance. When authority dominates unchecked, thought habits become rigid. When authority is rejected entirely, thinking becomes ungrounded. Maturity lies in integration.

Re-training authority-shaped thought habits requires emotional as well as cognitive adjustment. The discomfort associated with questioning authority must be tolerated. New experiences of safety while thinking independently must be created. Over time, the mind learns that inquiry does not equal danger. Thought becomes freer not through rebellion, but through understanding.

Ultimately, authority shapes thought habits by teaching the mind what to trust, what to fear, and what to ignore. These lessons are learned through repetition, emotion, and consequence. Recognizing this influence restores agency. Authority no longer dictates thinking automatically; it becomes one factor among many. The mind moves from obedience to discernment.

Chapter 5

Language and Internal Dialogue

Language is not merely a tool for communication; it is a primary instrument of thought. Long before ideas are analyzed or evaluated, they are shaped, framed, and constrained by words. The mind does not think in raw experience alone—it thinks in language, symbols, and narratives. As a result, the structure of language quietly governs the structure of thought, and internal dialogue becomes one of the most powerful forces shaping mental habits.

From early childhood, language provides the templates through which reality is interpreted. Words label experiences, categorize emotions, and assign meaning to events. Once something is named, it becomes easier to recognize—and harder to see differently. Language simplifies complexity, allowing the mind to operate efficiently. However, this efficiency comes at a cost. What language highlights becomes prominent; what it excludes fades from awareness. Thinking follows the paths language makes available.

Internal dialogue emerges as external language is absorbed and internalized. What begins as instruction, commentary, or evaluation from others gradually becomes self-talk. Over time, the mind learns to speak to itself using familiar phrases, judgments, and explanations. This internal dialogue feels personal, yet it is often composed of inherited language rather than original insight. Thoughts repeat not because they are carefully reasoned, but because the words that shape them are readily available.

Internal dialogue does more than describe experience; it directs attention and emotion. The way an event is narrated internally determines how it is felt. A situation framed as a threat produces anxiety. The same situation framed as a challenge produces motivation. Language acts as a filter through which experience is processed. Once a narrative is established, emotion follows predictably.

Repetition plays a central role in stabilizing internal dialogue. Frequently used phrases become cognitive shortcuts. They activate entire networks of assumptions and expectations instantly. Over time, these shortcuts harden into default interpretations. The mind no longer examines the language it uses; it thinks through it automatically. Habitual language produces habitual thought.

Importantly, internal dialogue often masquerades as objective reasoning. Because it unfolds silently and continuously, it feels like neutral observation. In reality, it is interpretive and selective. It emphasizes certain aspects of experience while ignoring others. When internal dialogue is rigid or repetitive, thinking becomes constrained within narrow narratives. The mind repeats conclusions rather than exploring possibilities.

Emotion amplifies this effect. Language linked to strong emotional experiences becomes especially influential. Words associated with shame, fear, pride, or validation are rehearsed frequently, strengthening their impact. Each repetition reinforces the emotional response, making the language feel increasingly accurate. Over time, emotional familiarity is mistaken for truth.

Social and cultural influences shape internal dialogue as well. Common phrases, moral judgments, and explanatory frameworks are absorbed from the surrounding environment. These linguistic patterns become internal reference points. The individual experiences them as personal beliefs, even though they originated externally. Language carries culture into the mind.

Internal dialogue also plays a critical role in self-concept. The stories individuals tell themselves about who they are, what they can expect, and how the world works are constructed linguistically. These stories are reinforced through repetition and memory. Once established, they guide perception and behavior automatically. Thinking becomes aligned with identity rather than evidence.

This chapter examines language not as a neutral medium, but as an active force in mental conditioning. By understanding how words shape thought, how internal dialogue forms, and how repetition reinforces narratives, we begin to see why certain thoughts feel inevitable. Language trains the mind to think along familiar lines, often without awareness.

Recognizing the power of language creates opportunity. When internal dialogue becomes visible, it becomes flexible. Words can be examined, questioned, and replaced. Thinking does not require eliminating language, but becoming conscious of how it is used. The mind can learn new ways of narrating experience—ways that invite reflection rather than repetition.

To change how we think, we must first understand how we talk to ourselves. Language is not just something we use; it is something that uses us. This chapter explores how internal dialogue becomes habit—and how awareness can transform it into a tool for intentional thinking rather than automatic repetition.

Words as Tools of Mental Framing

Words do not merely describe reality; they shape it. Every word carries assumptions, boundaries, and implications that influence how an experience is perceived, interpreted, and remembered. When the mind encounters a situation, it does not engage with raw reality directly. It engages with reality through language. Words act as tools of mental framing, defining what is emphasized, what is ignored, and how meaning is constructed. Over time, these frames become habitual, guiding thought automatically.

Mental framing refers to the way language structures perception. A single event can be understood in radically different ways depending on the words used to describe it. An obstacle can be framed as a problem or as a challenge. A mistake can be framed as a failure or as feedback. Each frame directs attention toward certain interpretations and away from others. The experience itself does not change; the mental response does.

The power of words lies in their ability to compress complexity. Reality is multifaceted and ambiguous. Language simplifies it into manageable categories. This simplification allows the mind to function efficiently, but it also limits perspective. Once an experience is framed linguistically, alternative interpretations become less accessible. The mind tends to operate within the frame provided, mistaking it for reality itself.

Framing begins early in life. Children learn how to interpret experiences by adopting the language used around them. When emotions are labeled repeatedly in certain ways, children learn not only how to describe feelings, but how to experience them. A child who hears anger described as dangerous may experience anger as threatening. A child who hears curiosity framed as disobedience may experience questioning as risky. Words do not merely label experience; they train emotional and cognitive responses.

Internal dialogue is where framing becomes most powerful. Once external language is internalized, the mind begins to narrate experience continuously. This narration happens so quickly and automatically that it feels like direct perception rather than interpretation. The individual does not notice the frame; they notice only the conclusion. Over time, the repeated use of certain words creates stable mental lenses through which all experience is filtered.

Labels are among the strongest framing tools. When a person labels an experience, behavior, or identity, the label activates a network of associations. Calling an event a "disaster" immediately invokes expectations of loss, blame, and distress. Calling the same event a "setback" suggests temporary difficulty and recovery. The label determines emotional response before reasoning begins.

Words also shape causality. The language used to explain why something happened influences responsibility and expectation. Phrases such as "this always happens to me" frame experience as inevitable and personal. Phrases such as "this happened under these conditions" frame it as situational and changeable. Over time, causal language trains beliefs about control, agency, and possibility.

Metaphors play a particularly influential role in mental framing. Metaphors translate abstract experiences into concrete imagery. When life is described as a battle, problems become enemies and effort becomes combat. When life is described as a journey, problems become obstacles or lessons. Metaphors are not decorative language;

they are cognitive structures that guide interpretation and behavior. The mind reasons through metaphor without realizing it.

Emotionally charged words have disproportionate impact. Words associated with fear, shame, or pride activate emotional memory networks. These words frame experience quickly and powerfully. Once an emotional frame is activated, alternative interpretations are suppressed. The mind seeks coherence with the frame rather than accuracy. Repetition strengthens this effect, making emotional language feel increasingly factual.

Social and cultural contexts reinforce framing through shared language. Societies develop preferred frames for success, failure, morality, and identity. These frames are embedded in everyday speech, media, and institutions. Individuals absorb them through repetition. Over time, culturally dominant frames feel like common sense. Thinking aligns with shared language rather than independent evaluation.

Framing also influences attention. Words direct focus toward specific aspects of experience. If a situation is framed as risky, attention scans for danger. If it is framed as an opportunity, attention scans for benefit. What is noticed reinforces the frame, creating a feedback loop. The mind sees what the words prepare it to see.

Importantly, framing affects memory. Experiences are remembered according to how they were framed at the time and during recall. A memory framed negatively is more likely to be recalled with distress. Each recall reinforces the frame, not necessarily the original event. Over time, the memory becomes a linguistic construct shaped by repeated narration rather than a neutral record.

Framing also shapes moral judgment. Words influence how actions are evaluated. Describing behavior as “assertive” versus "aggressive" or "disciplined" versus "controlling" leads to different moral conclusions. The evaluation often feels objective, but it is guided by language. Moral certainty frequently rests on framing rather than reflection.

The mind prefers familiar frames because they reduce cognitive effort. New frames require reorganization of meaning, which feels uncomfortable. As a result, people often resist reframing even when it would lead to better understanding. Familiar words feel true because they are easy. Unfamiliar frames feel wrong because they require effort. This resistance is neurological, not logical.

Recognizing words as tools of mental framing restores agency. When individuals become aware of the language shaping their thoughts, they can pause before accepting conclusions. This pause creates space for alternative frames. The goal is not to eliminate language, but to use it deliberately. Words can be chosen to open thinking rather than close it.

Reframing does not mean positive thinking or denial. It means accurate thinking. It involves selecting words that reflect complexity rather than exaggeration, specificity rather than generalization. For example, replacing "I failed" with "this attempt did not work" changes the frame from identity to process. The emotional response shifts accordingly, making learning possible.

Over time, deliberate reframing can retrain mental habits. New language patterns create new cognitive pathways. What initially feels forced can become natural through repetition. The same mechanism that once entrenched limiting frames can be used to establish more flexible ones. Language becomes a tool rather than a trap.

However, reframing must be grounded in honesty. Words that distort reality to avoid discomfort ultimately undermine trust in thinking. Effective framing aligns language with evidence while remaining open to nuance. It neither catastrophizes nor minimizes. It describes rather than judges. Such language supports clarity rather than defense.

Ultimately, words shape thought by defining the boundaries of interpretation. They determine what feels possible, what feels threatening, and what feels true. By understanding words as tools of mental framing, individuals gain the ability to examine their internal dialogue critically. Thinking becomes less reactive and more intentional. The mind no longer accepts every conclusion language presents; it learns to ask how the frame was built. In doing so, language becomes a means of understanding rather than a mechanism of repetition.

The Power of Labels and Definitions

Labels and definitions are among the most powerful instruments shaping human thought. They appear simple and harmless—mere words used to describe people, experiences, or events—but their influence reaches far beyond description. Labels do not only name reality; they organize it, constrain it, and guide interpretation. Once a label is applied, it frames how information is processed, how emotion is activated, and how future experiences are understood. In this way, labels function as cognitive shortcuts that quietly train the mind to think in predictable patterns.

A label is a compressed conclusion. It takes a complex set of traits, behaviors, or circumstances and reduces them to a single term. This compression is useful because it allows the mind to function efficiently. Without labels, every experience would require fresh analysis. However, efficiency comes at a cost. When complexity is reduced to a label, nuance is lost. The mind stops examining details and begins responding to the category itself.

Definitions deepen this effect by stabilizing meaning. A definition tells the mind not only what something is called, but what it is supposed to mean. Once a definition is accepted, it becomes a reference point for interpretation. Experiences are filtered through it automatically. Over time, definitions feel objective and self-evident, even though they are human constructions shaped by culture, authority, and repetition.

Labels strongly influence perception. When an individual is labeled as "difficult," "gifted," "lazy," or "successful," subsequent behavior is interpreted through that lens. Actions that fit the label are noticed and remembered, while contradictory actions are minimized or ignored. This selective perception reinforces the label, creating a self-confirming loop. The label feels accurate because the mind has been trained to see evidence for it.

Self-labels are especially influential. When people describe themselves using fixed labels, those labels shape identity. A person who defines themselves as "bad at math" or "not creative" narrows their perceived possibilities. The label becomes a boundary. Effort feels futile because the conclusion has already been drawn. The mind does not explore beyond the definition it has accepted.

Emotion intensifies the power of labels. Labels associated with shame, pride, fear, or belonging carry emotional weight. Once emotionally charged, a label becomes resistant to challenge. Questioning it feels threatening, not because it is true, but because it has become tied to self-worth or safety. The mind defends the label as if it were a fact rather than an interpretation.

Definitions also shape causality. How a problem is defined determines what solutions are considered. If an issue is defined as a personal failure, solutions focus on self-correction or blame. If the same issue is defined as a systemic challenge, solutions shift toward context and structure. The facts may be identical, but the definition directs thinking along entirely different paths.

Labels simplify moral judgment. By categorizing people or actions as "good," "bad," "right," or "wrong," the mind avoids deeper evaluation. Moral labels provide certainty and emotional closure. However, they also discourage understanding. Once a moral label is applied, inquiry often stops. The mind feels it has already reached a conclusion.

Social and cultural systems rely heavily on labels. Institutions categorize individuals to manage complexity. These categories then shape opportunity, expectation, and treatment. Over time, institutional labels are internalized. People begin to see themselves through the categories assigned to them. The label becomes a lens through which life is experienced.

Language repetition strengthens this process. The more often a label is used, the more familiar it becomes. Familiarity creates fluency, and fluency feels like truth. A label repeated in media, conversation, and internal dialogue gradually loses its appearance as a label and begins to feel like reality itself. The mind no longer distinguishes between description and fact.

Definitions can also freeze dynamic processes. Human behavior is fluid and context-dependent, yet labels imply stability. When a temporary state is labeled as a permanent trait, growth is obscured. A moment of fear becomes "an anxious person." A period of confusion becomes "unintelligent." The label replaces the process, and thinking becomes fixed.

The brain prefers labels because they reduce cognitive load. Evaluating each situation individually requires effort. Labels allow rapid response. However, reliance on labels shifts thinking from observation to assumption. The mind reacts to the category rather than the present reality. Over time, this habit limits adaptability.

Labels influence memory as well. Experiences are remembered according to how they were labeled. Once an event is defined in a certain way, recall reinforces that definition. Each retelling strengthens the label's authority. The memory becomes less about what happened and more about how it was categorized. This process stabilizes belief but distorts understanding.

Definitions are often inherited rather than chosen. Cultural language provides ready-made categories for interpreting experience. These categories feel natural because they are learned early and reinforced socially. Rarely do individuals examine the definitions they use. They think with them, not about them. This invisibility gives definitions their power.

Authority plays a critical role in establishing definitions. When definitions come from respected sources—experts, institutions, traditions—they are less likely to be questioned. The mind equates authority with accuracy. Once accepted, these definitions guide thinking automatically. Challenging them feels risky, even when evidence suggests revision is necessary.

However, definitions are not immutable truths. They are tools. Like any tool, their value depends on how they are used. Some definitions clarify; others constrain. Some support understanding;

others preserve bias. Effective thinking requires recognizing when a definition is serving understanding and when it is replacing it.

Reframing labels is a powerful way to change thinking. When a label is replaced with a more precise description, perception shifts. For example, replacing "failure" with "unsuccessful attempt" shifts focus from identity to process. The emotional response changes, making learning possible. Reframing does not deny reality; it describes it more accurately.

Removing labels entirely is not the goal. Without labels, communication would collapse. The goal is flexibility. Labels should be provisional, not absolute. They should invite revision rather than demand loyalty. When the mind treats labels as hypotheses instead of conclusions, thinking becomes more open.

Awareness is the first step. Noticing when a label is being applied—internally or externally—creates distance. This distance allows questioning. What does this label assume? What does it ignore? What alternative definitions might exist? These questions reintroduce critical reasoning into automatic thought.

Over time, deliberate use of language can retrain mental habits. Choosing descriptive language over evaluative labels encourages observation rather than judgment. Precision replaces exaggeration. Thought slows down enough to reflect. The same mechanism that once locked thinking into rigid categories can be used to create openness.

Ultimately, labels and definitions shape thought by defining the boundaries of meaning. They determine what is seen, remembered, and expected. When unexamined, they limit understanding. When examined, they become powerful tools for clarity. Mastery of thinking requires mastery of language. By understanding the power of labels and definitions, individuals regain the ability to think beyond the categories they inherited and to choose meanings that reflect reality rather than restrict it.

How Self-Talk Reinforces Thought Cycles

Self-talk is the continuous stream of inner language through which the mind interprets experience, evaluates events, and narrates reality. It operates quietly, often unnoticed, yet it plays a central role in shaping how thoughts repeat, strengthen, and become habitual. Self-talk does not merely reflect thinking; it actively trains it. Through repetition, emotional reinforcement, and narrative structure, self-talk reinforces thought cycles that can either support clarity and growth or trap the mind in predictable loops.

At its core, self-talk is learned language turned inward. What begins as external instruction, feedback, praise, criticism, and explanation gradually becomes internal dialogue. Over time, the mind adopts familiar phrases and patterns, using them automatically to make sense of situations. Because this dialogue feels internal and constant, it is experienced as personal truth rather than learned habit. The mind does not question it; it listens to it.

Self-talk reinforces thought cycles through repetition. Thoughts that are verbalized internally are more likely to recur. Each repetition strengthens the associated neural pathways, making the thought easier to access in the future. Over time, frequently rehearsed statements become default interpretations. The mind returns to them automatically, not because they are accurate, but because they are familiar.

The structure of self-talk also matters. Many internal statements are absolute, generalized, or identity-based. Phrases such as "this always happens," "I am not good at this," or "people cannot be trusted" close inquiry rather than open it. They present conclusions rather than observations. Each time such a statement is repeated, it reinforces a closed loop. The mind stops exploring alternatives and returns to the same conclusion.

Emotion amplifies this process. Self-talk linked to strong emotion is especially reinforcing. Thoughts accompanied by fear, shame, pride, or relief activate emotional memory systems, increasing repetition. A thought that reduces anxiety by providing certainty—even false certainty—is rewarded with emotional relief. The brain registers this relief as success, reinforcing the thought. Over time, self-talk becomes emotionally self-sustaining.

Self-talk also shapes attention. Internal dialogue directs focus toward specific aspects of experience. If self-talk emphasizes threat, attention scans for danger. If it emphasizes inadequacy, attention searches for failure. What is noticed then confirms the self-talk, reinforcing the cycle. The mind sees evidence for what it repeatedly tells itself.

Memory plays a critical role in this reinforcement. Self-talk often references the past to justify present conclusions. Each time a memory is recalled through internal dialogue, it is reconstructed and strengthened. The memory becomes aligned with the narrative being rehearsed. Over time, the past appears to confirm the self-talk, even when the memory has been selectively reconstructed to fit it.

Self-talk also reinforces identity. Repeated internal statements about who one is or what one can expect become embedded in self-concept. Once a thought becomes identity-linked, challenging it feels threatening. The mind defends it not because it is true, but because it feels defining. Thought cycles persist because they have been tied to the sense of self.

Importantly, self-talk is often mistaken for reasoning. Because it unfolds in language, it feels analytical. In reality, much self-talk is interpretive rather than evaluative. It explains rather than examines. When self-talk dominates thinking, conclusions are reached quickly and repeated without scrutiny. The mind confuses narration with understanding.

Self-talk also inherits social and cultural language. Internal dialogue often echoes phrases absorbed from authority figures, peers, and media. These phrases carry embedded assumptions and judgments. When repeated internally, they feel personal, even though they originated externally. Cultural scripts become private thought loops.

Negative self-talk is particularly reinforcing because it often masquerades as realism. Critical or pessimistic statements may feel honest or protective. In reality, they are often exaggerated interpretations that have been repeated until they feel factual. The emotional intensity attached to them increases their persistence. The mind confuses familiarity with accuracy.

Positive self-talk can also reinforce cycles, both helpful and unhelpful. Encouraging internal language can support motivation and resilience when grounded in reality. However, when positive self-talk denies evidence or suppresses doubt, it can create brittle confidence. The key is not positivity or negativity, but accuracy and flexibility.

Stress intensifies reliance on self-talk. Under pressure, the brain defaults to habitual patterns. Internal dialogue becomes faster, more rigid, and more repetitive. Nuance disappears. The mind seeks closure rather than exploration. Stress reveals which thought cycles have been most reinforced over time.

Self-talk also explains why insight alone rarely changes thinking. Understanding that a thought is inaccurate does not stop the internal narration that reinforces it. Each repetition of the self-talk strengthens the old pathway. Change requires altering the dialogue itself, not merely disagreeing with it intellectually.

Interrupting self-talk is the first step in weakening thought cycles. Noticing the language being used introduces distance. This distance creates choice. Instead of accepting the statement as truth, the mind can treat it as a hypothesis. This shift alone reduces automatic reinforcement.

Replacing self-talk does not mean silencing it. Silence is rarely sustainable. The mind needs language. The goal is to shift from evaluative, absolute language to descriptive, specific language. For example, replacing "I always fail" with "this attempt did not work" changes the frame from identity to process. The emotional response shifts accordingly, reducing reinforcement of the old cycle.

Repetition is essential for change. New self-talk must be practiced consistently to compete with established patterns. Initially, it feels unnatural and effortful. Over time, repetition strengthens new pathways. What once required conscious effort becomes automatic. The same mechanism that entrenched old thought cycles establishes new ones.

Emotional reinforcement must also change. New self-talk must be associated with meaningful outcomes—clarity, relief, understanding, or progress. Without emotional reward, new patterns will not persist. The brain learns through consequence, not intention.

Self-compassion plays a crucial role in this process. Harsh self-talk often persists because it has been reinforced through fear or shame. Introducing compassion reduces emotional threat, allowing the mind to explore alternative narratives safely. Safety enables flexibility. Without it, self-talk remains defensive.

Ultimately, self-talk reinforces thought cycles because it is the voice through which repetition occurs. The mind becomes what it repeatedly tells itself. This process is not a flaw; it is a learning mechanism. When unexamined, it creates rigid patterns. When understood, it becomes a powerful tool for intentional thinking.

By bringing self-talk into awareness and reshaping it deliberately, individuals gain the ability to alter their mental habits. Thoughts no longer repeat by default; they are guided by choice. The inner voice shifts from automatic narrator to reflective guide. In doing so, thinking becomes less reactive, less repetitive, and more aligned with reality rather than habit.

Thinking in Narratives, Not Facts

Human beings do not naturally think in isolated facts. They think in stories. Experiences are not stored or processed as neutral data points; they are organized into narratives with causes, meanings, intentions, and conclusions. This narrative structure is how the mind makes sense of complexity. While facts describe what happened, narratives explain why it happened and what it means. Over time, these narratives become the primary drivers of belief, judgment, and behavior, often overshadowing factual accuracy.

Narrative thinking is efficient. Reality presents an overwhelming amount of information at any given moment. If the mind attempted to process each detail independently, it would become paralyzed. Narratives reduce complexity by linking events together into coherent sequences. They create beginnings, middles, and endings. They assign roles such as victim, hero, cause, and consequence. This organization allows the mind to function smoothly, but it also introduces distortion.

Facts are static. Narratives are dynamic. A fact can exist without meaning, but a narrative always carries interpretation. When the mind encounters an event, it does not stop at observation. It immediately begins constructing a story: what led to this, what it says about me, what it implies about others, and what will likely happen next. This story feels like understanding, even when it is built on assumptions rather than evidence.

Emotion is the engine of narrative thinking. Facts alone rarely persist in memory unless they are embedded in emotionally meaningful stories. Emotion provides motivation, relevance, and continuity. As a result, the mind favors narratives that explain emotional experience, even when those narratives oversimplify or exaggerate. A story that makes emotional sense feels more true than a fact that lacks meaning.

Narratives also satisfy the mind's need for coherence. Uncertainty is uncomfortable. Randomness is unsettling. Narrative provides order by turning coincidence into causality and ambiguity into intention. When events are framed as part of a story, the mind experiences relief. The cost of this relief is accuracy. The mind prefers a coherent explanation over an incomplete one, even if the explanation is flawed.

Memory reinforces narrative dominance. Experiences are remembered not as raw footage, but as stories that have been told and retold. Each retelling strengthens the narrative structure while altering or discarding factual detail. Over time, the memory becomes the story, not the event. What is recalled feels consistent and reliable, even when it has drifted significantly from what actually occurred.

Narrative thinking also shapes identity. Individuals understand themselves through personal stories: who they are, what they deserve, what kind of person they have been, and what kind of future they can expect. These identity narratives guide interpretation automatically. New experiences are filtered through existing stories. Evidence that fits the narrative is accepted; evidence that contradicts it is reinterpreted or dismissed.

Social environments amplify this process. Groups share narratives about history, morality, success, and failure. These shared stories create collective meaning and cohesion. Over time, group narratives feel like facts because they are repeated, validated, and emotionally reinforced. Questioning them feels disruptive, not because the facts are solid, but because the story is stabilizing.

Language is the primary vehicle of narrative thinking. Words link events, assign motives, and establish cause-and-effect relationships. Phrases such as "because," "always," "never," and "that means" transform observation into story. Once language frames an event narratively, alternative interpretations become less accessible. The mind moves from seeing to explaining without pause.

Narratives also influence moral judgment. Facts describe actions; narratives assign blame or virtue. When behavior is placed into a moral story, evaluation feels complete. The mind no longer asks what happened; it believes it knows who someone is. This shortcut simplifies social interaction but undermines fairness and understanding.

Importantly, narratives feel personal even when they are inherited. Cultural, familial, and institutional stories are absorbed gradually through repetition. Over time, they become internal frameworks. Individuals experience them as their own beliefs, unaware of their origins. Narrative thinking becomes automatic, not chosen.

Narratives are resistant to change because they organize meaning. Challenging a narrative threatens coherence, identity, and emotional stability. Even strong factual evidence may fail to alter belief if it disrupts the story. The mind defends narratives not because they are true, but because they are familiar and stabilizing.

Critical reasoning operates differently. It isolates facts from interpretation. It asks what is known, what is assumed, and what is uncertain. Narrative thinking blends these elements together. The result feels like understanding, but it is often conclusion without examination. This is why people can argue passionately from narratives that contain few verifiable facts.

The media environment intensifies narrative dominance. Information is presented as stories with clear arcs and emotional hooks. Complexity is reduced to conflict. Repetition strengthens familiarity, and familiarity feels like truth. The mind absorbs stories faster than it evaluates facts.

Narratives are not inherently harmful. They are necessary for meaning-making and communication. The danger arises when narratives replace facts rather than organize them. When stories become immune to evidence, thinking becomes rigid. Growth requires the ability to revise narratives in response to reality.

Awareness is the first step toward balance. Noticing when a conclusion is narrative-based rather than evidence-based creates distance. Questions such as "What are the facts?" and "What story am I telling?" reintroduce reasoning into automatic thought. This does not eliminate narrative thinking, but it subjects it to examination.

Effective thinking integrates narrative and fact. Facts ground understanding; narratives provide context. When narratives remain flexible and evidence-responsive, they support insight. When they become fixed and defensive, they distort perception.

Ultimately, the mind thinks in narratives because stories make life intelligible. But intelligibility is not the same as truth. Understanding the difference allows individuals to hold stories lightly and facts carefully. Thinking becomes less about defending meaning and more about discovering reality.

Chapter 6

Emotion as a Thinking Accelerator

Emotion is often portrayed as the enemy of rational thought—a disruptive force that clouds judgment and overrides logic. This view misunderstands emotion's true role in thinking. Emotion does not replace thought; it accelerates it. It speeds up perception, interpretation, and decision-making by prioritizing certain information and suppressing others. Rather than slowing the mind down, emotion propels it forward—often faster than conscious reasoning can keep pace.

At a biological level, emotion exists to guide action. Long before humans developed complex analytical reasoning, emotional responses helped organisms decide what mattered. Threats demanded immediate attention. Opportunities required quick engagement. Emotion evolved as a shortcut system, allowing rapid evaluation without exhaustive analysis. In modern thinking, this system remains deeply embedded. Emotion tells the mind what is urgent, relevant, or dangerous before facts are fully processed.

Because emotion accelerates thinking, it shapes conclusions early in the cognitive process. When an emotional response is triggered, interpretation follows its direction. Fear narrows attention toward risk. Anger focuses it toward blame or injustice. Desire highlights possibility and reward. These emotional signals do not wait for evidence; they frame evidence as it arrives. By the time conscious reasoning begins, the direction of thought has often already been set.

This acceleration explains why emotionally charged thoughts feel immediate and certain. There is little sense of deliberation because emotion reduces perceived need for it. The mind experiences emotional clarity as insight. In reality, it is speed masquerading as understanding. The faster a conclusion is reached, the more convincing it feels—especially when supported by strong emotion.

Emotion also determines which thoughts repeat. Experiences paired with emotional intensity are remembered more vividly and recalled more frequently. Each recall reinforces both the emotion and the interpretation attached to it. Over time, emotionally reinforced thoughts become default responses. The mind does not revisit them to evaluate; it activates them automatically. Emotion trains repetition.

Importantly, emotion does not discriminate between accurate and inaccurate interpretations. A belief that reduces anxiety may be emotionally rewarded even if it distorts reality. A narrative that explains pain may persist because it provides emotional resolution, not because it reflects truth. The brain prioritizes emotional regulation over objective accuracy. Emotion accelerates thinking toward comfort and certainty.

Emotion also compresses complexity. Under emotional activation, nuance fades. The mind favors clear categories and decisive judgments. Ambiguity becomes intolerable. This narrowing of thought is adaptive in urgent situations, but problematic in complex ones. Emotion speeds up thinking by simplifying it, often at the expense of depth.

Social emotion further amplifies this process. Feelings such as belonging, rejection, pride, or shame accelerate thought in group contexts. Beliefs aligned with group identity feel emotionally safe and are adopted quickly. Beliefs that threaten belonging provoke discomfort and are resisted. Emotion accelerates conformity by tying thought to social survival.

Understanding emotion as a thinking accelerator reframes its role. The problem is not emotion itself, but unexamined acceleration. When emotion sets the pace of thought without awareness, conclusions harden prematurely. When emotion is recognized and regulated, it can inform thinking without dominating it.

This chapter explores how emotion speeds up thinking, reinforces repetition, and shapes belief formation. By understanding emotion's accelerating function, we gain insight into why certain thoughts feel immediate, compelling, and resistant to change. Emotion is not opposed to thinking—it is one of its most powerful engines. The task is not to eliminate emotion from thought, but to learn when to slow it down.

Why Emotional Thoughts Repeat More Often

Emotional thoughts have a unique persistence in the human mind. They return uninvited, replay themselves with intensity, and resist dismissal even when they are unhelpful or outdated. This repetition is not accidental, nor is it a failure of self-control or intelligence. Emotional thoughts repeat more often because they are neurologically prioritized, psychologically reinforced, and functionally tied to the brain's core survival and learning systems. The mind is not designed to treat all thoughts equally; it is designed to amplify what feels emotionally significant.

At the most fundamental level, emotion signals importance. When an experience triggers emotion—fear, anger, shame, joy, or desire—the brain interprets it as meaningful. Meaning, in evolutionary terms, is information that may affect survival, safety, or social standing. As a result, emotionally charged thoughts receive preferential treatment. They are encoded more strongly, recalled more easily, and activated more quickly than neutral thoughts.

Emotion accelerates attention. When an emotional response is activated, the brain narrows focus toward the perceived source of that emotion. This attentional narrowing increases cognitive resources devoted to the thought. The more attention a thought receives, the more neural activation it generates. Repeated activation strengthens neural pathways, making the thought easier to trigger again. Over time, emotional thoughts become the mind's default responses.

Memory systems are deeply intertwined with emotion. Experiences accompanied by strong emotion are consolidated more robustly in memory. The brain releases neurochemicals that enhance plasticity during emotional events, strengthening the connections associated with those experiences. This does not mean emotional memories are more accurate; it means they are more accessible. Accessibility, not truth, determines repetition.

Recall further amplifies emotional thought repetition. Each time an emotional memory is recalled, it is reactivated and reconsolidated. During this process, the emotional tone is often preserved or even intensified. The memory is not simply retrieved; it is rewritten. If the recall is accompanied by distress, fear, or rumination, the emotional association grows stronger. The brain learns that this thought still matters.

Emotional thoughts also repeat because they often lack resolution. The brain dislikes unfinished business. When an emotional experience has no clear conclusion—no explanation, closure, or sense of control—the mind continues to revisit it. Replay becomes an attempt to resolve uncertainty. Until the emotional system signals safety or understanding, the thought remains active.

Fear-based thoughts are particularly repetitive. Fear evolved as a rapid-warning system. When a threat is detected, the brain encodes cues associated with that threat so they can be recognized quickly in the future. Even when the original threat is gone, similar cues can trigger the same fear response. The brain prefers false alarms to missed danger. Emotional repetition is the cost of protection.

Shame and guilt-based thoughts also persist because they are tied to social survival. Human beings evolved in groups where acceptance meant safety. Experiences involving rejection, humiliation, or moral failure are treated as high-priority information. The mind replays these events to prevent future social harm. Each replay strengthens the association between the situation and emotional pain, increasing repetition rather than resolution.

Pleasure-driven emotional thoughts repeat for a different reason. Reward reinforces behavior and expectation. Thoughts associated with pleasure, relief, or validation are rehearsed because they signal opportunity. The brain replays them to recreate or pursue similar outcomes. Repetition strengthens desire and anticipation, shaping motivation and preference.

Emotional thoughts are also more linguistically rehearsed. People tend to talk—internally and externally—about emotional experiences more than neutral ones. Storytelling, rumination, and internal dialogue transform emotion into narrative. Each narration reinforces the memory and its emotional meaning. Over time, the story becomes more stable and more accessible, even if it becomes less accurate.

Emotion creates feedback loops with attention and interpretation. An emotional thought directs attention toward confirming information. That information reinforces the emotional belief, which increases emotional intensity. The loop sustains itself. Neutral or contradictory information receives less attention and is less likely to interrupt the cycle.

Stress further intensifies emotional thought repetition. Under stress, the brain prioritizes speed over accuracy. Habitual patterns dominate. Emotional thoughts that have been reinforced in the past rise to the surface automatically. The mind does not explore alternatives; it returns to what is familiar. Stress reveals which emotional patterns are most deeply trained.

Importantly, emotional thoughts often masquerade as insight. Because emotion creates clarity and urgency, the thought feels important and true. The mind interprets intensity as validity. This misinterpretation reinforces repetition. The individual believes the thought must be addressed again because it feels unresolved or meaningful, even when replay produces no new understanding.

Emotional thoughts also become identity-linked. Repeated emotional narratives about the self or the world solidify into self-concept. Once a thought becomes part of identity, it is defended automatically. Challenging it feels like a threat to the self. The mind repeats it not to examine it, but to preserve coherence.

Suppression increases repetition. When individuals attempt to push emotional thoughts away without processing them, the brain interprets the suppression as evidence of importance. Monitoring for the thought paradoxically keeps it active. Emotional thoughts repeat not because they are indulged, but because they are resisted without integration.

Insight alone rarely stops emotional repetition because insight operates at a different level than reinforcement. Emotional thoughts are strengthened by activation, not belief. Knowing that a thought is irrational does not weaken the neural pathways that support it. The brain changes through repeated experience paired with emotional regulation, not through logical dismissal.

Reducing emotional thought repetition requires slowing the acceleration process. Emotional regulation allows the brain to re-evaluate the thought without reinforcing it. When emotional intensity decreases, the memory becomes more flexible. New interpretations can be introduced during recall, altering reconsolidation. Over time, the thought loses priority.

Replacing emotional thought cycles does not mean eliminating emotion. It means changing the emotional consequences of repetition. When reflection leads to clarity rather than distress, new pathways are reinforced. The brain learns that the thought no longer requires urgency. Repetition decreases naturally.

Compassion plays a critical role in this process. Many emotional thoughts persist because they are tied to fear or shame. Harsh self-judgment reinforces emotional intensity. Compassion reduces threat, allowing the mind to disengage from defensive repetition. Safety enables flexibility.

Ultimately, emotional thoughts repeat more often because emotion is the brain's relevance signal. The mind returns to what it believes matters. This mechanism is not a flaw; it is a learning system designed to protect and adapt. The problem arises when emotional priority outlives its usefulness.

Understanding why emotional thoughts repeat restores agency. It reframes repetition as trained significance rather than personal failure. With awareness, emotional regulation, and deliberate reinterpretation, the same mechanisms that once entrenched repetition can be used to release it. Emotional thoughts fade not when they are fought, but when the brain learns they no longer require urgent attention.

Fear, Pleasure, and Survival-Based Thinking

Human thinking did not evolve to discover truth in the abstract. It evolved to keep the organism alive. Long before logic, philosophy, or science, the brain's primary task was survival. Fear and pleasure emerged as the core signaling systems guiding this task. These emotional forces did not simply influence behavior; they shaped how thinking itself developed. Modern thought still operates on this ancient foundation. Much of what feels like reasoning is, at its core, survival-based thinking driven by fear and pleasure.

Fear and pleasure function as directional signals. Fear pushes the mind away from perceived threats. Pleasure pulls it toward perceived rewards. Together, they create a motivational compass that guides attention, memory, interpretation, and decision-making. This system operates faster than conscious reasoning because survival required speed. A delayed response to danger or opportunity could be fatal. As a result, fear and pleasure accelerate thought by simplifying it.

Fear-based thinking narrows cognition. When fear is activated, the brain shifts into protective mode. Attention becomes selective, scanning for threat-related cues. Ambiguity is reduced. Nuance fades. The mind favors certainty over complexity because certainty enables rapid action. This narrowing is adaptive in dangerous situations, but it distorts thinking in modern contexts where threats are often symbolic rather than physical.

Under fear, the brain prioritizes worst-case scenarios. This bias is intentional. From a survival perspective, overestimating danger is safer than underestimating it. The cost of a false alarm is minor compared to the cost of ignoring a real threat. As a result, fearful thoughts repeat easily. The brain rehearses them to ensure readiness. The repetition is not pessimism; it is preparation.

Fear-based thinking also strengthens memory. Experiences associated with fear are encoded deeply so similar situations can be recognized quickly in the future. This mechanism explains why negative or threatening experiences feel more vivid and intrusive. The mind replays them not because it enjoys suffering, but because it is trying to prevent recurrence. Unfortunately, when the environment changes, this mechanism can misfire, producing chronic anxiety or rumination.

Pleasure-based thinking operates differently but is equally powerful. Pleasure signals opportunity, reward, and resource acquisition. When pleasure is anticipated or experienced, the brain reinforces the thoughts and behaviors that led to it. These thoughts are rehearsed because they promise benefit. The mind becomes oriented toward repetition of what felt good, safe, or relieving.

Pleasure-based thinking often creates attachment to outcomes. When a certain belief, behavior, or interpretation produces pleasure or relief, it becomes preferred. The brain learns not to question it too closely. Accuracy becomes secondary to reward. This is why comforting beliefs persist even when evidence contradicts them. The pleasure of certainty outweighs the discomfort of doubt.

Fear and pleasure together shape habit formation. Thoughts that reduce fear or increase pleasure are reinforced. Thoughts that increase fear or reduce pleasure are avoided. Over time, the mind learns which thinking patterns are emotionally efficient. These patterns become automatic, not because they are correct, but because they are effective at regulating emotional states.

Survival-based thinking explains why logic often fails to change beliefs. Logical arguments operate slowly and require cognitive effort. Fear and pleasure operate instantly and emotionally. When a belief is tied to safety or reward, challenging it triggers threat responses. The brain defends the belief not because it has been reasoned, but because it has been emotionally reinforced.

This mechanism also explains why people cling to familiar suffering. Known pain is predictable; unknown change is not. Fear prefers certainty, even if it is unpleasant. The mind may repeatedly return to negative thoughts because they feel safer than uncertainty. Letting go of a familiar narrative feels risky because it removes the illusion of control.

Survival-based thinking also shapes moral judgments. Actions are evaluated based on perceived threat or benefit rather than objective principles. Fear frames others as dangerous or untrustworthy. Pleasure frames alignment as good or virtuous. Moral certainty often arises from emotional alignment rather than ethical reasoning. The mind concludes first, then justifies.

Social survival amplifies these dynamics. Humans evolved in groups where belonging was essential. Fear of exclusion and pleasure of acceptance strongly influence thought. Beliefs that align with group norms feel safe. Beliefs that threaten belonging provoke anxiety. Survival-based thinking encourages conformity not through logic, but through emotional signaling.

Modern environments intensify survival-based thinking. Continuous exposure to threat-related information, competition for attention, and reward-based feedback systems keep fear and pleasure activated. The brain is repeatedly signaled that something urgent or desirable is happening. Thought accelerates constantly. Reflection becomes difficult because the system rarely returns to baseline.

Importantly, survival-based thinking is not irrational. It is context-sensitive. The problem arises when ancient mechanisms operate in environments they were not designed for. Symbolic threats—social judgment, uncertainty, abstract risk—trigger the same responses as physical danger. The mind reacts as if survival is at stake when it is not.

This mismatch explains why emotional thoughts feel urgent even when no action is required. Fear demands resolution. Pleasure demands repetition. Both create momentum. The mind feels compelled to think, decide, or act immediately. Slowing down feels uncomfortable because it contradicts survival programming.

Understanding survival-based thinking reframes emotional repetition. Persistent thoughts are not failures of discipline; they are expressions of deeply ingrained adaptive systems. Fear and pleasure are doing what they evolved to do. The task is not to eliminate them, but to recognize when they are misapplying urgency.

Regulating survival-based thinking requires restoring distinction between real threat and perceived threat. This does not happen through argument, but through experience. When the mind repeatedly encounters situations where feared outcomes do not occur, fear loses priority. When pleasure is decoupled from rigid beliefs, flexibility increases.

Slowing thinking is essential. Fear and pleasure accelerate cognition; awareness decelerates it. Naming emotional activation creates distance. When the mind recognizes, "This is fear speaking," or "This is reward-seeking," it interrupts automatic reinforcement. The thought loses some of its urgency.

Developing tolerance for uncertainty is critical. Survival-based thinking seeks closure. Reflective thinking accepts ambiguity. When the mind learns that uncertainty is not dangerous, fear-driven repetition decreases. This learning must be experiential, not conceptual.

Ultimately, fear and pleasure shape thinking because they are the brain's original guidance system. They direct attention, reinforce memory, and accelerate conclusions. These mechanisms once ensured survival; today, they shape belief, identity, and repetition. Understanding their role restores balance. Thinking becomes less reactive and more intentional—not by rejecting emotion, but by placing it in its proper role. Emotion remains a signal, not a commander.

Mood-Driven Perception and Bias

Human perception is not a neutral recording of reality. It is an interpretive process shaped continuously by internal states, especially mood. Mood acts as a background filter that colors how information is noticed, interpreted, remembered, and evaluated. While people often believe they are responding to the world as it is, they are more often responding to the world as it feels. Mood-driven perception quietly biases thinking, influencing judgments and reinforcing habitual thought patterns without conscious awareness.

Mood differs from emotion in duration and scope. Emotions are typically brief and tied to specific triggers; mood is more diffuse and enduring. Because mood persists, it subtly influences a wide range of perceptions rather than a single reaction. A person in a low mood may interpret neutral events negatively, while the same events appear benign or even positive in a lighter mood. The external situation remains unchanged, yet the perceived meaning shifts.

This occurs because mood primes the brain's interpretive systems. When a particular mood is active, it increases the accessibility of mood-consistent thoughts and memories. This phenomenon, known as mood-congruent processing, causes the mind to retrieve information that matches its current state. When someone feels anxious, past threats come to mind. When someone feels content, memories of safety and success surface. The mind does not search for balance; it searches for coherence with mood.

Mood-driven bias begins with attention. Mood influences what the mind notices first and most strongly. In a negative mood, attention gravitates toward problems, risks, and imperfections. In a positive mood, attention shifts toward opportunities, solutions, and strengths. This selective attention creates a feedback loop. What is noticed reinforces the mood, which further guides attention. Perception becomes self-validating.

Interpretation is the next stage of bias. Once information is noticed, mood shapes what it means. Ambiguous situations are especially vulnerable. A delayed response from someone else can be interpreted as rejection in a low mood or as neutrality in a stable one. The mind fills gaps in information using mood-consistent assumptions. These assumptions feel reasonable because they align with internal state.

Memory further entrenches mood-driven perception. Experiences encoded during a particular mood are more easily recalled when that mood returns. Over time, memory becomes organized around emotional states rather than objective timelines. This organization gives the impression that "things are always this way," when in fact the mind is sampling selectively from mood-matched memories. The past appears to confirm the present mood.

Mood-driven bias also affects judgment. People in negative moods tend to make harsher evaluations of themselves and others. Mistakes appear larger, risks appear greater, and outcomes appear less controllable. Conversely, positive moods can produce overconfidence, underestimation of risk, and overly optimistic projections. In both cases, mood distorts accuracy by shifting thresholds of evaluation.

Importantly, mood biases are experienced as insight rather than distortion. Because mood operates continuously, its influence feels invisible. People attribute their conclusions to reasoning rather than state. A pessimistic judgment feels like realism; an optimistic judgment feels like clarity. The mind rarely asks whether the conclusion would feel the same in a different mood.

Mood also influences the speed of thinking. Negative moods often slow cognition, leading to rumination and fixation. Positive moods can accelerate thinking, promoting broad associations but sometimes reducing scrutiny. Neither state guarantees accuracy. Each produces characteristic biases that favor certain types of conclusions.

Stress intensifies mood-driven perception. Under stress, mood becomes more dominant because cognitive resources are reduced. The brain relies more heavily on heuristics and familiar interpretations. Nuance diminishes. The mind defaults to mood-consistent explanations because they require less effort. This is why stress often magnifies existing biases rather than creating new ones.

Social perception is especially affected. Mood shapes how others' intentions are inferred. In low moods, ambiguous behavior is interpreted as hostile or dismissive. In positive moods, the same behavior is interpreted as neutral or benign. These interpretations influence interaction, often eliciting responses that reinforce the original perception. The bias becomes interpersonally validated.

Mood-driven bias also influences belief formation. Repeated judgments made under similar mood states harden into beliefs. Over time, the belief appears stable, even though it was formed through repeated mood-influenced evaluations. The individual believes they have learned something objective about the world, when they have learned something about their recurring mood patterns.

This process explains why some beliefs persist despite contradictory evidence. If evidence is encountered during a mood that discounts it, it fails to register fully. The belief survives because it is reinforced during dominant mood states. The mind's sampling of reality is biased by how it feels at the moment of sampling.

Mood also shapes moral perception. Actions are judged more harshly during negative moods and more leniently during positive ones. What feels unforgivable one day may feel understandable another. These fluctuations are rarely recognized as mood-based. Moral certainty feels absolute, even when it is state-dependent.

Importantly, mood-driven perception is not pathological; it is adaptive. Mood evolved to signal environmental conditions. Low mood encourages caution and analysis; positive mood encourages exploration and engagement. Problems arise when mood is chronic or when its influence is unrecognized. What was once adaptive becomes limiting.

Awareness is the primary antidote to mood-driven bias. Recognizing that perception is state-dependent introduces humility into judgment. Questions such as "Would this look different if I felt calmer?" or "What am I noticing because of how I feel?" slow automatic interpretation. This pause creates space for correction.

Separating observation from interpretation is critical. Noticing raw facts before assigning meaning reduces mood intrusion. Facts remain relatively stable across moods; interpretations do not. By distinguishing the two, the mind reduces bias without suppressing emotion.

Regulating mood also reduces perceptual distortion. Adequate rest, emotional processing, and stress reduction return the brain closer to baseline. When mood intensity decreases, perception becomes more flexible. This flexibility allows alternative interpretations to be considered.

Experience plays a key role. When individuals observe that the same situation appears different across moods, they learn not to trust immediate conclusions fully. This learning weakens the authority of mood-driven judgments. Over time, perception becomes less reactive.

Ultimately, mood-driven perception reveals that thinking is not purely cognitive; it is embodied and emotional. Bias does not arise from flawed reasoning alone, but from unrecognized state influence. Understanding this restores agency. Mood can inform thinking without dominating it.

By recognizing mood as a lens rather than a verdict, individuals gain the ability to think more accurately. Perception becomes something to examine rather than obey. The world remains complex, but thinking becomes more balanced—not because emotion is eliminated, but because its influence is understood.

Conclusion

Thinking Is Trainable

Thinking often feels automatic, personal, and fixed. Thoughts arise quickly, interpretations feel immediate, and conclusions seem self-evident. Yet throughout this book, a different picture has emerged—one that challenges the idea that thinking is a static trait or an inherent talent. Thinking is not a fixed capacity; it is a trained pattern. What feels natural is usually what has been practiced, reinforced, and repeated over time.

The mind learns how to think in the same way it learns how to walk, speak, or respond emotionally—through exposure, repetition, feedback, and consequence. Experiences shape neural pathways. Emotions assign priority. Language frames meaning. Memory reinforces patterns. Social environments reward some interpretations and discourage others. Over years of repetition, these influences solidify into habits of thought that feel automatic and unquestionable. The mind repeats what it has learned to repeat.

Understanding this reframes responsibility without assigning blame. Persistent thought patterns are not evidence of weakness, lack of intelligence, or flawed character. They are evidence of training. The mind adapted to its environment exactly as it was designed to do. Thoughts that once reduced fear, gained approval, or provided certainty were reinforced. Over time, they became defaults. What once served survival may no longer serve growth, but the mechanism itself is neutral.

This perspective also explains why insight alone rarely produces lasting change. Knowing that a thought is inaccurate does not immediately dismantle the pathways that support it. Thinking changes through activation, not intention. The brain learns through repetition paired with emotional consequence. Old patterns weaken only when they are no longer rehearsed and rewarded. New patterns strengthen only when they are practiced consistently and experienced as meaningful.

Thinking is trainable because the brain remains plastic. Neural pathways are not permanent structures; they are living systems shaped by use. Attention strengthens what it repeatedly activates. Language organizes what the mind returns to. Emotion reinforces what feels important. By engaging these same mechanisms intentionally, thinking can be reshaped.

Training thinking does not mean controlling every thought or eliminating emotion. It means becoming aware of how thought patterns form and choosing how to engage them. It involves slowing down automatic conclusions, questioning familiar narratives, and distinguishing observation from interpretation. It means noticing how mood, fear, pleasure, authority, and language accelerate thinking—and learning when to let them inform judgment and when to pause them.

Crucially, training thinking requires tolerance for discomfort. New ways of thinking feel unfamiliar and effortful at first. Old patterns feel easier because they are well-worn. Discomfort is not a sign that new thinking is wrong; it is a sign that the brain is working differently. Growth occurs not by avoiding discomfort, but by allowing it without retreating into familiar conclusions.

Repetition is essential. Just as unhelpful thought cycles were trained through repetition, more accurate and flexible thinking must be trained the same way. Reflective self-talk must be practiced. Nuanced language must replace rigid labels. Emotional regulation must accompany reinterpretation. Each repetition strengthens a new pathway. Over time, what once required effort becomes natural.

Social environments matter as well. Thinking is easier to retrain in contexts that reward curiosity, uncertainty, and reflection rather than certainty and conformity. Where possible, surrounding oneself with dialogue rather than dogma supports mental flexibility. Where this is not possible, internal permission to question becomes even more important.

Training thinking is not about achieving perfect objectivity. Human cognition will always be influenced by emotion, memory, and context. The goal is not purity, but awareness. A trained mind recognizes its own tendencies. It treats conclusions as provisional rather than final. It remains open to revision in light of new evidence or new understanding.

Ultimately, recognizing that thinking is trainable restores agency. Thoughts are no longer fate; they are habits. Habits can be changed—not quickly or effortlessly, but reliably, through practice. The mind is not a prison built by the past; it is a system shaped by experience and capable of reshaping itself.

When thinking becomes intentional rather than automatic, repetition gives way to reflection. Familiar narratives loosen their grip. Emotion informs without commanding. Language clarifies rather than confines. The mind remains human—patterned, emotional, and social—but it becomes more flexible, accurate, and free.

Thinking is not something you either have or lack. It is something you practice. And whatever has been practiced can be practiced differently.

www.ingramcontent.com/pod-product-compliance
Lightning Source LLC
Chambersburg PA
CBHW041300210926
51847CB00009B/84
9789699797286